READY-TO-USE ACTIVITIES AND MATERIALS ON
DESERT INDIANS

A Complete Sourcebook for Teachers K-8

READY-TO-USE
ACTIVITIES AND MATERIALS ON
DESERT INDIANS

A Complete Sourcebook
for Teachers K-8

DANA NEWMANN

NATIVE AMERICANS RESOURCE LIBRARY

VOLUME 1

**THE CENTER FOR APPLIED
RESEARCH IN EDUCATION**
West Nyack, New York 10994

10 9 8 7 6 5 4 3 2 1

Production Editor Zsuzsa Neff

Interior Design by Audrey Kopciak

Library of Congress Cataloging-in-Publication Data

Newmann, Dana.
    Ready-to-use activities and materials on desert Indians : a complete
sourcebook for teachers K-8 / Dana Newmann.
        p.   cm. — (Complete Native Americans resource library : v. 1)
    Includes bibliographical references.
    ISBN 0-87628-607-4 (alk. paper)
    1. Indians of North America—Sourthwest, New—Study and teaching
(Elementary) 2. Indians of North America—Southwest, New—Study and
teaching—Activity programs. I. Title. II. Series.
E76.6.N48   1995 vol. 1
[E78.S7]
978'.00497'00712 s—dc20
[978'.00497'00712]   95-33118
                                                            CIP

ISBN 0-87628-607-4

THE CENTER FOR APPLIED
RESEARCH IN EDUCATION
A division of Simon & Schuster
West Nyack, New York 10995

Printed in the United States of America

THIS BOOK IS DEDICATED TO MARIE ORLINDA CORIZ
WITH MUCH AFFECTION AND ADMIRATION

ABOUT THE AUTHOR

A graduate of Mills College in Oakland, California, Dana Newmann has been an elementary teacher for more than 15 years. She has taught in California and New Mexico and for the U.S. Army Dependents Group in Hanau, Germany.

Mrs. Newmann has authored a variety of practical aids for teachers including *The New Teacher's Almanack* (The Center, 1980), *The Early Childhood Teacher's Almanack* (The Center, 1984), and *The Complete Teacher's Almanack* (The Center, 1991).

She presently lives in Santa Fe, New Mexico, where for the past six years she has worked for Project Crossroads, a nonprofit educational resource organization. Mrs. Newmann heads the elementary school program and conducts workshops for teachers throughout the state and the Southwest.

Photo credit: Gail Rieke

ABOUT THE NATIVE AMERICAN REVIEWERS OF THIS BOOK

Ella Jones was born in Fort Defiance, Arizona, on the Navajo reservation, and Navajo is her first lanuage. For many years she was associated with Little Earth School (Pre-K through 4) in Santa Fe, New Mexico, where she lives today with her husband Richard and their two children, Brendan and Valerie.

Abby Moquino, born in Santo Domingo Pueblo taught for 10 years at the American Indian Art Institute in Santa Fe. Recently she began teaching highshool students in Bernalillo, NM where many of her students are from her home pueblo.

Today Abby and her 3 children, Trisha and twins Hayes and Valie live in Cochiti Pueblo, New Mexico.

A FEW WORDS
ABOUT THE NATIVE AMERICANS
RESOURCE LIBRARY

The *Native Americans Resource Library* is a four-book series that introduces you and your students in grades K-8 to the lives of the peoples who have inhabited North America for thousands of years. The four books in this *Resource Library* are:

- Ready-to-Use Activities and Materials on *Desert Indians (Unit I)*
- Ready-to-Use Activities and Materials on *Plains Indians (Unit II)*
- Ready-to-Use Activities and Materials on *Coastal Indians (Unit III)*
- Ready-to-Use Activities and Materials on *Woodland Indians (Unit IV)*

Each unit in the series is divided into the following sections:

- "Their History and Their Culture"—Here you'll find information about the historical background of the particular region ... food ... clothing ... shelter ... tools ... language ... arts and crafts ... children and play ... religion and beliefs ... trade ... social groups and government ... when the Europeans came ... the native peoples today ... historic Native Americans of the particular region.
- "Activities for the Classroom"—Dozens of meaningful activities are described to involve your students in creating and exploring with common classroom materials: native shelters, tools, jewelry, looms; also included are directions for making and playing traditional Native American games; foods of the particular region ... and *much* more!
- "Ready-to-Use Reproducible Activities"—These are 30 full-page worksheets and activity sheets that can be duplicated for your students as many times as needed. The reproducible activities reinforce in playful and engaging ways the information your students have learned about a particular region.
- "Teacher's Resource Guide"—You'll find lists of catalogs, activity guides, professional books, and children's books covering the specific region you are studying.

Throughout each book in the series are hundreds of line drawings to help illustrate the information. A special feature of each book are the many historic photographs that will help "bring to life" the Native American tribes as they were in the 19th and early 20th centuries!

The *Native Americans Resource Library* is designed to acquaint you and your students with this important and complex subject in a direct *and* entertaining way, encouraging understanding and respect for those people who are the *first* Americans.

A NOTE FROM THE AUTHOR
ABOUT THIS BOOK

Sharing the information contained in this book with the general public schools is something that is long overdue. It gives "in-sight" information and is written so the young children can understand and appreciate it. The more we know of other people's cultures, the better we can live and work together. After all, we are all "little children" of the Mother Earth. I hope the teachers will take to heart this marvelous book when they teach this material; and enjoy it as well. I enjoyed reading this material.

I appreciate what Dana Newmann has done in developing this book. I believe the information on the Navajo is as accurate as can be.

—Ella Natonabah Jones,
Navajo reviewer of this book

The descendants of the peoples who lived on this continent before the Europeans arrived have come to be known as Native Americans. This term is perhaps more accurate than Indians which can be confusing based as it was on Christopher Columbus's mistaken idea that he had arrived at islands off of India.

In this book you will look at the lives of Native Americans of the Southwest: who they are, how they arrived here, and how they have organized their lives for the many centuries they have been in the desert region. Then you will consider the effects of the arrival of the Europeans to the southwest and will look at contemporary Native American life in this area.

Occasionally present-day Native American life is cited in the history sections. This is because in organizing this material, it became clear that in each section there are overlaps between the life and activities of desert Indians historically and the way they live today. This emphasizes the continuity of attitudes and thought that has existed for them over the centuries.

Today it is essential that students realize their way of life is not solely the creation of 20th-century people. Much of what we eat and use, and much that is beautiful, has been given to us by the first inhabitants of this land. Our children should understand this, so this book will help you and your students learn of the specific gifts we have received from Native Americans.

This particular Native American culture is based on each person having respect for all living things; it emphasizes what it means to live in harmony with one's surroundings. These are two essential lessons for each of us to teach—and to learn—as we enter the 21st century.

Today about one-third of all Native Americans live in the Southwestern United States.   Each group—including Pueblo, Navajo, Apache, Pima, Maricopa, Papago, Havasupai—is distinct in certain ways from all the others. This is an area rich in information and I have worded these materials in simple terms so that they may be understood and enjoyed by *all* your students.

This book offers a first glimpse into a vastly rich and complex culture. I hope it will be an exciting beginning for you and your class as you explore Native American studies—together!

Dana Newmann

CONTENTS

THE DESERT INDIANS:
THEIR HISTORY AND THEIR CULTURE
1

THE DESERT INDIANS:
READY-TO-USE REPRODUCIBLE ACTIVITIES
121

LOWER GRADES, EASIEST ACTIVITIES

MIDDLE GRADES

UPPER GRADES, MORE CHALLENGING ACTIVITIES

DESERT INDIANS: TEACHER'S RESOURCE GUIDE
159

RESOURCE LIST 161

BIBLIOGRAPHY 164

THE
DESERT INDIANS

Their History
and Their Culture

PREHISTORY

Between a million and half a million years ago there were at least four times when large areas of the earth were covered with ice.

Sometime toward the end of the last great glaciers—some 25,000 years ago—Mongolian people began to move across the Bering Strait which was then a land bridge. They walked the 55 miles from Siberia to Alaska—and became the very first North Americans![1]

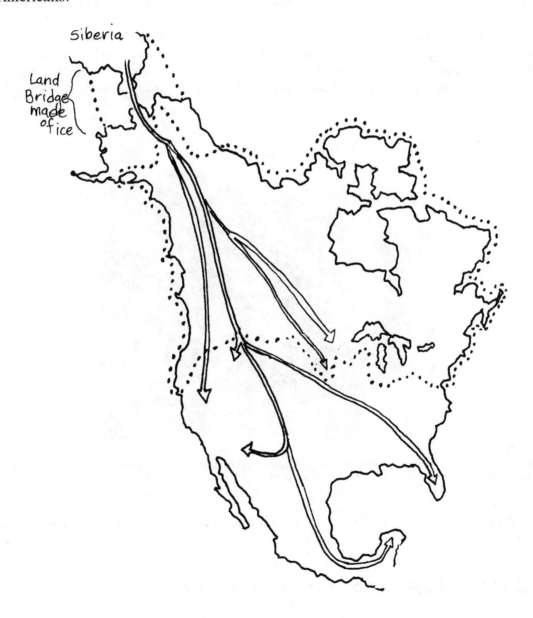

Over the next centuries the descendants of these people would continue moving southward until they populated the continents of both North and South America—all the way from Alaska to Tierra del Fuego.

When we speak of the Southwest we mean the southwestern area of the United States which today includes the southern parts of present-day Utah and Colorado, on down through Arizona and New Mexico, and including the western part of Texas.

The topography of the Southwest is varied: southern Colorado has flat-topped mesas and deep canyons, the Mogollon Mountains of New Mexico are sharp-edged, and there are arid deserts—the Painted and Sonoran—as well.

But there is one constant in the Southwest and that is the climate. It is arid with less than a five-inch average annual rainfall, most of which occurs in a six-week period in the summer.

Depending on altitude and rainfall, the vegetation includes mainly western evergreen, piñon, juniper, chamisa, cactus, and mesquite. (See Photo 1.) This land may be sparse in vegetation, yet it is the oldest continually inhabited area of North America! Here 12,000 years ago the Mongolian hunter stalked the giant mastodon.

Photo 1. Sotol and "Fingers" on road to Paradise near Portal, Arizona; November 8, 1963 *Photo by Henry D. Tefft. Courtesy Museum of New Mexico (neg. no. 123927)*

Present-day Native Americans of the Southwest are descended from various tribal people who came into this area from the north, south, and eastern parts of the continent.

THE MOGOLLON (C. 300 B.C.–C. A.D. 1300)

The first well-known group in this area was the Mogollon (Moh-go-yohń), named for the small mountain range where they lived along the southern border of present-day Arizona and New Mexico. They arrived in the area in about 300 B.C.

Although they did some farming, the Mogollon were at first hunter-gatherers, living on nuts, seeds, roots, and locusts. Their farming methods were simple and involved the use of the digging stick; their crops included squash, beans, tobacco, corn, and cotton. (Because they farmed, the Mogollon lived in permanent settlements, in well-insulated pit-houses built 3 to 4 feet into the ground.)[2] Their villages were always near a stream and supported at most 30 houses and perhaps 200 people.

The Mogollon knew how to weave and they made blankets and clothing from woven cotton, animal hair, and feathers. They used a fire-drill and made pitch-lined baskets for boiling food. Their pottery was among the first in the Southwest and had no decoration until about A.D. 700 when they came in contact with the Hohokam who are described below. Eventually they produced unique decorated bowls (Mimbres pottery, named for

Photo 2. Food bowls. *Courtesy Museum of New Mexico (neg. no. 28365).*

the river along which it was made) that showed abstracted animals and people in daily life and ritual and that often exhibited the artist's sense of playfulness. (See Photo 2.) The Mogollon created turquoise and shell necklaces and worked stone, wood, and bone.

Probably theirs was a slow decline and by about A.D. 1250 or 1300 the Mogollon had been absorbed by the Anasazi to the north. Today, the Zuni Indians of New Mexico are considered by archaeologists, based on artifacts, to be the descendants of the Mogollon.

THE HOHOKAM (C. 100 B.C-C. A.D. 1500)

The Hohokam (Hoh-hoh-kahm) or "Vanished Ones" in the Pima language probably came north from Mexico in about 100 B.C. and settled in the Salt and Gila River Valley areas of Arizona where they dug hundreds of miles of narrow irrigation ditches and lined these with clay to prevent seepage. Their earthen dams had woven mat flood gates. The Hohokam had an elaborate irrigation system that brought water from as far off as the Gila River, some 30 miles away. They raised large fields of corn, beans, squash, tobacco, and cotton. Their main village, called Snaketown by archaeologists, had 100 pit houses, covered 300 acres, and was inhabited for 1,500 years!

The Hohokam were active traders and borrowed much from their southern neighbors including corn, cotton, the making of copper bells, and certain pottery styles. The Hohokam were a peaceful people who left not race of war or violence. They created mosaic pyrite mirrors and elaborate textiles and they are believed to have invented the etching of shells process about A.D. 1100.

We do not know why the Hohokam eventually abandoned Snaketown and their other villages. Perhaps drought or repeated invasions drove them away. But in about A.D. 1500 the Hohokam left in small bands, scattering throughout the Southwest.

Today the Pima and Papago Indians are believed by archaeologists, based on artifacts, to be descended from those early Hohokam, the "Vanished Ones."

THE ANASAZI (C. 100 B.C.–C. A.D. 1300)

The third important culture of the early Southwest and the one to become the most advanced was that of the Anasazi (On-uh-saw´-zee) which means "Ancient Ones"* in the Navajo language.

---

*Literally translated Anasazi is Navajo for "Our Old Enemies" and for this reason the Hopis have requested that their ancestors now be referred to as: Ancestral Puebloan peoples. (Source: New Mexico Park Services.)

Living to the northeast of the Hohokam and Mogollon (where present-day Utah, Arizona, Colorado, and New Mexico meet), the Anasazi settled close by rivers or springs and within the drainage basin of the San Juan River.

The earliest Anasazi are called "the Basketmakers." They developed weaving in about 100 B.C. and created baskets[3], sandals, mats, and traps from yucca fibers, rushes, vines and straw. At first, they lived in brush enclosures or in caves. They were hunters, using the spear-thrower, *atl-atl* (ah́-tl-ah́-tl), and eventually the more efficient bow and arrow. They began raising corn and drying the excess kernels which they stored in round mud-lined brush-covered pits in the floors of their caves. They were a peaceful people and fought only if attacked.

By about A.D. 500–700 the Basketmakers began to create pottery by laying coils of clay one on top of the other—much as their yucca baskets were formed. They also began building thatch-roofed pit houses and by A.D. 750 they were making adobe and stone buildings.

Then in about A.D. 1030 "the Basketmaker" culture turned into "the Cliff Dweller" when the Anasazi joined the small adobe buildings together, creating multi-storied apartment complexes, walled cities, and cliff-dwellings built of shaped and mortared sandstone.

These huge constructs had up to 800 rooms and could house thousands of residents. This radical new building style is today called Pueblo[4] architecture. (See Photo 3.)

Photo 3. North building of Taos Pueblo; circa 1920. *Photo by T. Harmon Parkhurst. Courtesy Museum of New Mexico (neg. no. 12470).*

Though they never dug large irrigation canals, the Anasazi found ingenious ways of watering their crops: they planted gardens in the sand at the foot of long sloping rocks beneath their cliff dwellings. There, any runoff could gently seep through the sand to nurture their plants. Sometimes they terraced hillsides, slowing runoff and redirecting it to their crops, or they dammed streams and flooded their acres of corn.

They cultivated small fields of red corn, beans, and sunflowers (for their seeds), growing these plants side by side in each row.

Because of their successful farming techniques, the Ancient Ones had the time and freedom to develop their arts. This is why from about A.D. 1030–1300 the Anasazi lived in a Golden Age! They created elaborate woven feather and cotton textiles. They had bracelets, beads, buttons, needles, combs, brushes, whistles, canes, and dice. They made intricately painted pottery, fabulous baskets, and mosaic jewelry; they also developed a rich religious life with awe-striking rites and ceremonies.

The Anasazi organized vast trade routes that they marked at night with enormous bonfires. Traders brought them salt from Zuni Lakes, seashells from California and Mexico, turquoise from Galisteo Basin, and macaws, parrots, and feathers from South America.

Then suddenly in about A.D. 1300 the Anasazi abandoned their fabled cliff cities, sometimes leaving pottery, blankets, tools, or food in those empty rooms. Why did they all leave in this mass departure? We will probably never be certain.

There are some speculations. Which one seems the most likely to you? Perhaps continual raids by the nomadic Apaches and Navajos had weakened the Anasazi until they were forced to disperse, *OR* it may have been that their elaborate trade route system became overlarge until it collapsed, leaving them stranded without the trade materials to which they had become accustomed, *OR* the depleted wood supply (there were no trees for 40 miles around Pueblo Bonito) had made cooking and heating on the cliffs just too difficult, *OR,* as many archaeologists believe and the tree rings from that period substantiate, the 23-year drought they suffered from A.D. 1276–1299 may have made it impossible for the Anasazi to raise food and forced them to leave their homes. Whatever the true reason(s), the Anasazi moved off to the south where they established new, smaller pueblos and became the ancestors of modern-day Pueblo and Hopi Indians.

Two of the early Anasazi communities—Acoma (in New Mexico) and Oraibi (in Arizona)—were not completely abandoned. Today, there continues to be pueblo villages both at Acoma and at Oraibi. These two villages are believed to be the oldest continually occupied sites in the United States.

RAIDERS FROM THE NORTH

From about A.D. 1000 small bands of people from the north migrated to the Southwest. These often warlike people, who lived by hunting and gathering seeds and nuts, were the ancestors of present-day Apaches and Navajo people. They were related to the Athabaskan-speaking tribes of Canada.

Eventually, they came to live near the Anasazi and the Pueblo peoples and raided their villages to gain food and goods. Both the Apache (uh-patch´-ee: *the Enemy* in Zuni) and the Navajo (nah´-vuh-hoh: a Spanish version of a Pueblo word meaning *big planted fields*) learned some farming from their Pueblo neighbors, but they continued to depend on hunting to supply most of their food. They lived mainly on rabbit, deer, and antelope and gathered roots, piñon seeds, and cactus fruits.

IN A NUTSHELL

The first people who came to the Southwest had one of two main ways of living: they either farmed or they moved around in search of food.

The farming people came 2,500 years ago. They raised corn, beans, squash, and cotton. They were peaceful and they made many wonderful baskets and beautiful pottery. Eventually, they built—often on cliffs—huge adobe and stone apartments, called *pueblos*, where a thousand people could live. Over many years' time they became the Pueblo Indians (the Hopi and Zuni) and the Pima and Papago Indians of today.

The early people who hunted and gathered seeds instead of farming came to the Southwest from the north about 1,000 years ago. They wandered about in search of rabbit, deer, antelope, nuts, seeds, and roots. They were fierce fighters and often raided the farmers for food or goods. These wandering people are the ancestors of the Apache and Navajo Indians of today.

Notes for "Prehistory":

1. Archaeologists believe this theory based on artifacts and bones found at campsites and killsites. However, many Native Americans do not believe this theory. They rely instead on their creation stories and songs which teach that "the people" emerged from the Sipapu, the center of the Earth, that their journey began in the north and that they continue their trek south.

2. Some of the buildings were larger than the houses and were used as social or ceremonial centers. The present-day Pueblo kivas (kee´-vahs), ceremonial underground buildings, are descended from these ninth-century structures.

3. These included burden and winnowing baskets, sifters, backpacks, tiny baskets as well as ones that were 4 feet tall and 240 feet long!

4. This Spanish word for "community" or "town" is used today to refer to an architectural style as well as to the Pueblo Indian people, inheritors of the Anasazi, or Ancestral Puebloan, culture!

All people, in all cultures, have the same basic needs: food to nurture their bodies, and clothing and shelter to protect them from heat, cold, and rain.

So it was with the early Native Americans also.

FOOD

Many of the foods eaten in the world today were first grown by Native Americans. Over 80 plants—including corn, pumpkin, squash, and many kinds of beans—were given to us by those early Southwestern people.

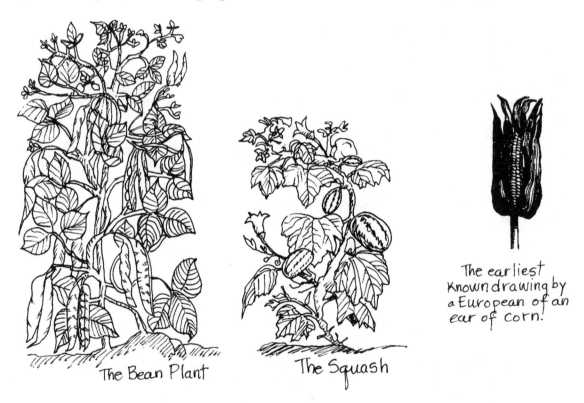

The Bean Plant

The Squash

The earliest known drawing by a European of an ear of corn.

In hot, dry areas like the Southwest, animals are small and scarce. This helps explain why the early people of this region ate mainly plants. The Native Americans of this region gathered berries, nuts, and bulbs, and ground seeds into flour.[1] When they did have meat to eat it was usually rabbit, birds, prairie dogs, or in some regions, fish.[2]

Many of these early people were accomplished farmers and raised pinto beans, squash, and corn. It was essential that their crops have water; the ancestors of today's Pueblo, Pima, and Hopi constructed irrigation systems to bring water to their fields. Many of their religious concerns reflect this involvement with the need for rain.

The Navajos believe that Changing Woman, the Earth Mother, gave them the gift of corn.

CORN[3]

Corn is a grain that grows in kernels on long ears. It was first grown in the New World. Tiny cobs, ears of corn, and corn paintings on pottery are often found in pre-Columbian burials in the Southwestern United States. The oldest ears of corn found in North America are 5,500 years old and were discovered at Bat Cave in west central New Mexico. A thousand-year-old popped kernel of corn was found in a dry cave in southwestern Utah. It had been popped by the ancestors of the present-day Pueblo people.

Corn made up as much as 80 percent of the early Southwest Native American's diet.

Those early people of the Southwest knew a great deal about the cultivation of corn, and the first European settlers adopted many of their techniques, including: planting corn in hills and among squash and beans for more rapid growth, using husking pegs when shucking corn, storing corn in airy cribs to prevent spoilage, roasting ears of green corn, and making hominy by soaking corn kernels in lye to remove the husks.

Much of the Hopi corn crop each year was dried and then ground into very fine cornmeal. (See Photo 4.)

Photo 4. Grinding corn in Zuni Pueblo; circa 1912. *Photo by Jesse L. Nusbaum. Courtesy Museum of New Mexico (neg. no. 28689).*

This was put into a flat basket and shaped into a tall cone. Then it could be made into *piki* (pee-kee), a roll made of wafer-thin (pale blue) sheets of cornmeal, which was the daily bread of the Hopi. To make *piki*, the finely-ground cornmeal was thinned with water and wood ash. A greased slab of sandstone, called a duma (doo´-mah) was heated from below by a fire. The baker dipped her hand into the cornmeal batter and spread it in a thin layer on the *duma*—this was done quickly, so as not to burn her hand. The batter baked in a moment, and then it was lifted by a corner, using the thumb and forefinger, and quickly rolled up into a cylinder while the sheet was still pliable.

Once cooled, the *piki* became crisp and could be eaten by itself, but it was best when dipped into a hot stew made of beans, squash, watercress, dandelions, milkweed and, for flavoring, wild sagebrush!

> *The corn grows up.*
> *The waters of the dark clouds drop, drop.*
> *The rain descends.*
> *The waters from the corn leaves drop, drop.*
> *The rain descends.*
> *The waters from the plants drop, drop.*
> *The corn grows up.*
> *The waters of the dark mist drop, drop.*
>
> —NAVAJO[4]

SQUASH

Summer squash is a quick-growing, small-fruited vine of the gourd family. Squash seeds from about 4000 B.C. have been found in Mexican caves. We get our word "squash" from the Algonquin Indians of Massachusetts who called the plant *askoot-asquash*. Squash is native to the New World, where early people grew it long before Christopher Columbus or the Spanish arrived.

The squash itself takes many shapes: long, crooked, pear-shaped, or round. It may be light green, yellow, or cream-colored. Squash grow quickly and must be picked just a few days after they form—before the skin and seeds have a chance to harden. Unless they are sliced and dried, squash must be eaten soon after they are picked, as they spoil quickly.

Winter squash, such as pumpkin, are usually large in size and take many months to mature. They can be stored for a long time if they are kept dry and above freezing.

BEANS

Beans were grown by the people of prehistoric times in North America. Pinto beans appeared in the Southwest in about 1000 B.C. They are called "pinto" as this is the Spanish word for "spotted." Such beans grow on an upright bush that has pods which are tough and full of fiber, so the pods are not eaten (as we do with green string beans). The beans, themselves, are the seeds inside the pods.

Once picked, the beans are taken out of the pods and dried. Later, they can be soaked in water and simmered with onions and a bit of meat—until they are soft enough to be eaten.

WILD FRUITS

Cactus fruits, agave, and yucca fruits were important wild food sources. Yucca fruit was roasted and eaten or dried and stored for use during the winter. Sometimes the fruit was made into a fermented beverage.

PINE NUTS

When the Spanish arrived in the Southwest they found small scrub pines that had edible seeds; they called this tree *piñon* (peen-yohn´). It takes 60 to 100 years for a piñon tree to mature. It produces little seeds with tough brown shells. The tiny kernel inside is white. Traditionally, early Native Americans would chew some of these kernels and feed this pulp to very young children. This was actually a good source of protein for their babies!

PRAIRIE DOGS

This small squirrel-like rodent of North America has cheek pouches, tiny ears, long front claws, strong hind legs, and a short strong tail. It eats plants, seeds, and insects. Prairie dogs live in large communities of interconnected burrows. They give a high piercing whistle to warn one another of approaching danger.

The early people of the Southwest sometimes trapped prairie dogs as a source of food.

DEER

Before going out to hunt deer, a man would make prayer offerings to the gods who protected the animal. Once a deer had been brought down by an arrow, the Pueblo hunter would run up and, lifting the animal's head, breathe into his own body the last breath of the slain deer, so that he and the animal were one. Then the hunter would thank the deer's spirit for giving up its life so that he and his family might eat and grow strong. Tiny down feathers were tied to the dead deer's antlers so that its spirit might reach "the clouds" more quickly.

TURKEYS

When Coronado's expedition first came to the Pueblo villages in 1540, the chronicler Castañeda noted "the cocks with great hanging chins"—turkeys! These native birds were being raised in pens as food (and for their decorative feathers).

It is said that at that time, Europeans thought of the East as a source of exotic things. So when these birds were first seen in Europe, people began referring to them as Turkey hens, and the first part of the name persists to this day.

SEASONINGS

Flavorings were created by the addition of seeds, grasses, and roots to the container of simmering main ingredients. Salt was received from traders who brought it from Zuni Lakes.

It is interesting to note that there were no tables in early pueblos. Meals eaten inside a pueblo dwelling were spread on the floor, where the people might remain close to Mother Earth who had provided the food.

Ceremonial meals in the pueblos today are also eaten on the floor to honor their early ancestors and the Earth itself.

Notes for "Food":

1. It is interesting to note that the Rio Grande area people were short in height: the men averaged 5 feet 4 inches, and the women just 5 feet. This lack of stature was likely due to the spare diets they had as children.

2. How do we know what people ate 5,000 years ago in the Southwest? Archaeologists have discovered evidence of corn, beans, rabbit, deer, piñon nuts, squash, and prairie dogs in prehistoric cave dwellings and burials.

3. The word "corn" first meant a seed or grain, e.g., *peppercorn* means "grain" of pepper, and *corned beef* was cured with "grains" of salt.

4. From the *Journal of American Folklore*, vii, 191, translation by Washington Matthews, reprinted with the permission of the American Folklore Society, Inc.

Photo 5. Oven. *Credit unknown.*

CLOTHING

The clothing of each group of Southwestern people reflected the natural materials that were available to them. Animal skins, yucca fibers, turkey feathers, and woven cotton threads all served as materials from which early people created their clothing.

APACHE-NAVAJO

The Apaches wore animal skins. The men had breechcloths of buckskin and leather leggings and foot covers. Their long, flowing hair was kept in place by a leather headband. (See Photo 6.)

Photo 6. Navajo scout; circa 1883. *Photo by Ben Wittick. Courtesy School of American Research Collections in the Museum of New Mexico (neg. no 15938).*

The early Navajo man wore moccasins made of deerskin, tanned with the animal's brains and dyed with plant dyes. When he wore these shoes he became a typical Navajo example of cooperation in the natural world among animal, plant, and the human being.

PUEBLO

The Hopi men hunted and used the hides of their game for making clothes. The leggings worn by both women and men were deerskin, and Hopi men often wore buckskin breechcloths. Rabbit fur headbands held down the men's bangs and wrapped around the *chongo* (chon´go: Spanish for hair knot, made when long hair is gathered into a thick flat cube worn wrapped at the back of the neck).

The Hopis grew cotton and wove it into short kilts for the men and calf-length women's blankets, which were worn draped under the left arm and tied at the right shoulder. (See Photo 7.)

Photo 7. Masha-honka and friend; Oraibi Pueblo of Hopi, Arizona; circa 1890. *Photo by Ben Wittick. Courtesy Museum of New Mexico (neg. no. 16204).*

Hopi women made robes woven from strips of rabbit skin. All other weaving was men's work and each man had to supply his family with clothing. The men harvested the cotton, carded it (raising the nap), and spun it into thread. The women dyed this thread golden yellow, orange, red, green, and black—all of these colors they took from native plants such as snakeweed, rabbit brush, or goldenrod for yellow; alder bark for red; Indian paintbrush for rust; sagebrush for brown; Navajo tea or brown onionskin for orange; the purple bee plant for lavender; juniper or mistletoe for tan; and Blue Flower Lupine for pale blue.

Most of the weaving was done during the winter months when the fields lay unplanted; old men who no longer worked the fields were free to weave all year round. Woven feather and string blankets were worn in winter to ward off the chill. Sandals made of woven yucca fiber have been found in many archaeological excavations. (Examples are shown in Photo 19 in **Arts and Crafts**.)

The people of the other Southwestern pueblos dressed in much this same manner. (See Photo 8.)

PIMA AND PAPAGO

Because these people lived in the hot, dry southlands, they had less need for body coverings.

Photo 8. San Juan Pueblo clothing; circa 1935. *Phot by T. Harmon Parkhurst. Courtesy Museum of New Mexico (neg. no. 4488).*

The men wore their hair in many tiny braids or shoulder length and free-flowing. Their chests were bare and a woven cotton or animal skin kilt covered a diaper-like wrapping beneath. A woven belt held up the kilt. A loose pancho-like covering would be used if night winds were chilly. Simple leather sandals covered the soles of their feet.

Tattoos were worn on the forehead and lower eyelids and face painting adorned the cheeks, temples, and chin. The Pima men wore a great deal of jewelry including shell anklets, rings, bracelets, earrings, and mosaic inlaid bone hair ornaments. (See Photo 9.)

The Pima and Papago women wore woven or skin skirts and sandals held up by leather thongs. They wore shell and stone beads, bracelets, rings, and necklaces.

Photo 9. Pima man and woman; circa 1882. *Photo by Ben Wittick. Courtesy Museum of New Mexico (neg. no. 102058).*

Note to the Teacher: As an introduction to the next section, **Shelter**, ask your students to brainstorm together a list of all the natural materials (they have heard mentioned in the **Food** and **Clothing** sections) from which early Southwest Native Americans could have constructed their shelters, e.g., cornstalks, branches, dirt, animal hides, and so on. Next, ask them to consider the climate in the Southwest and the conditions it imposed on the people. Then have them, singly or in small groups, try to invent dwellings for:

- **The Pima and Papago** (hunter-gatherers in the far south where it is dry, hot, and windy with sparse vegetation)
- **The Navajo** (sheepherders with some shelters near their small, tilled summer fields and a second set at some distance apart of more protected winter dwellings)
- **The Pueblo** (farmers, large groups of people who were sometimes attacked by nomadic tribes, extreme heat as well as cold winters)

Encourage originality and the use of any available natural materials such as mud, stones, vines, and yucca fiber. Ask your students to provide "details," e.g., type of roofing used, how rain, heat, wind were dealt with, and so on. Review all the final solutions and be generous in appreciating the individuality and creative problem-solving! Now they are ready to continue with the **Shelter** section itself!

SHELTER

As was the case with their clothing, early Southwestern people built their shelters from the materials offered by their natural surroundings: brush, mud, straw, rocks, willow and cottonwood saplings, tree trunks, bark, hay, and sandstone.

THE KI AND RAMADA OF THE PAPAGO AND PIMA

The Pima and Papago both built and lived in the *ki* (key), a structure based on bent branches. The Papago used willow and cottonwood to shape a large dome and then plastered this with a roof of adobe (a mixture of mud and straw). The Pima, who lived far to the south, used desert plants such as ocotillo (oh-koh-tee´-yoh) and saguaro (sah-gwah´-roh) cactus as the base of their *kis*, which were slightly sunken into the ground. These structures were extremely strong and could withstand raging winter winds. (See Photo 10.)

Photo 10. Papago wickiups; Arizona; circa 1915. *Courtesy Museum of New Mexico (neg. no. 21675).*

In the summer, arbors, also known by their Spanish name *ramadas* (rah-mah´-dahs), were built. They were made of brush-covered tree trunk supports and placed adjacent to the *kis* so that they could offer ventilation to the people. This was important because the temperature was often over 100 degrees F.

THE NAVAJO HOGAN

When the Navajos came to the Southwest in about A.D. 1025, they lived in makeshift shelters made of brushwood, skins, and leaves.

19

Once they became sheepherders, the Navajos built more permanent dome-shaped structures called *hogans* (hoh´-gons). *Hogan* means "home place" in the Navajo language. Navajos believe that Changing Woman built the first hogan from turquoise and shell. These early hogans were often located at the foot of cliffs or in box canyons. Constructed of timbers and poles covered by bark and dirt, these buildings were well insulated and waterproof. A smoke hole was placed directly over the open fire pit and allowed most of the smoke to rise and leave the living area. The door always faced the rising sun in the East, as that is the direction in which the Sun, sustainer of all life, appears each morning. Once the hogan was built, it was blessed so that all who lived in it might have a good life. (See Photo 11.)

Photo 11. Navajo ceremonial hogan north of Crownpoint, New Mexico; November 4, 1916. *Photo by Wesley Bradfield. Courtesy Museum of New Mexico (neg. no. 82428).*

"The Navajo House Blessing"

> *House made of winds*
> *House made of fur*
> *House made of pollens*
> *House made of flint*
> *House made of crystals*
> *Bless my house made of mud,*
> *   resin and pine.*
> *Bless my family made of blood,*
> *   marrow and bone.*[1]

The hogan symbolizes the coming together of all elements in Nature. It is made of plants (logs, branches, moss), animals (leather lashings), earth (mud), sacred elements (corn pollen is rubbed on the main rafters [*vigas*] (vee-gahs) during the hogan's blessing), and, finally, the hogan is lived in by humans.

Rather than forming towns or villages, the Navajos usually built loose clusterings of hogans scattered over a wide area. Navajos are very family-oriented and so they usually live in groupings with other family members including grandparents, aunts, and uncles.

PUEBLO-STYLE BUILDINGS

Among Pueblo people, building a house was a family matter, in which each person had a special role. The men brought the stones from a *mesa* (may´-suh), Spanish for "table" and referring to the huge flat-topped hills. The heavy wooden beams, *vigas*, were cut from pine forests, sometimes 60 miles away. The outline of the room to be built was sprinkled with sacred cornmeal, and eagle feathers were placed at each of the four corners to ensure that the new inhabitants of the house would have long and good lives. The foundation was rock topped by adobe-packed rubble.

Once the foundation was set, the women—using ladders—built the walls of fitted sandstone or adobe bricks. More adobe was used as mortar and to fill in any cracks. From time to time, work stopped and prayers were offered that the house have a strong foundation, that the walls remain solid, and that its inhabitants prosper.

After the walls were plastered, the men placed the *vigas* overhead, about two feet apart, to span the room. A second layer of lighter poles, *latillas* (lah-tee´-yahs) was laid across the *vigas*. These were followed by a layer of brush, one of hay, one of smoothed-out moist adobe—and once this had dried, the women raked dry earth over their now completed rooftop!

The large pueblo dwellings evolved from single storage rooms made of stone and adobe which grew into large single-family enclosures. Finally, the idea developed of grouping rooms together, placing them atop one another, and using ladders to connect various levels. Some of these levels became terraces, the roof of one building serving as the yard of the next. From about A.D. 1100 to 1300, elaborate apartment-type cliff dwellings were being built by the ancestors of present-day Pueblo people. (See Photos 12 and 13.)

Mesa Verde's "Cliff Palace" in Colorado had plazas, 220 rooms, 23 *kivas* (sacred underground rooms), and ceremonial towers. (See Photo 14.) One of the Great House complexes of Chaco Canyon in New Mexico, "Pueblo Bonito," was a D-shaped structure. Its arc faced into a huge opening in the canyon wall, where gardens and plazas were located. The outward facing back of the structure was flat, windowless, straight up—and, therefore, impenetrable. Pueblo Bonito had 37 kivas, as well as two Great Kivas, and it had 800 rooms for its inhabitants!

Photo 12. Spruce Tree House in Mesa Verde, Colorado. *Phot by McKee. Courtesy Museum of New Mexico (neg. no. 153977).*

Photo 13. Spruce Tree House in Mesa Verde, Colorado; circa 1908. *Photo by Jesse L. Nusbaum. Courtesy Museum of New Mexico (neg. no. 60595).*

Photo 14. Cliff Palace in Mesa Verde, Colorado. *Courtesy Museum of New Mexico (neg. no. 144622).*

Note for "Shelter":

1. "The Navajo House Blessing" translation is from *Song of the Tewa* by Herbert V. Spinden, published by The Exposition of Indian Tribal Arts, 1933.

TOOLS

We humans have been defined as "the tool-making animals." This ability sets us apart.

What is a tool? An extension of the hand, the arm, one's power. Tools are created to exert force, to pierce, to scrape, to collect, to cut, to hold, and to refine! The tools of early Native Americans demonstrate these qualities. They simplified the lives of early people—and made their lives sweeter.

FOR HUNTING

Atl-Atl (ah´-tl-ah´-tl)

The base of this weapon had a long groove into which the spear fit. The hunter held the atl-atl in his hand, parallel to the ground with his fingers in the loop. A quick snap of the wrist thrust the dart or spear into the air. The atl-atl lengthened the hunter's throw and was accurate from a distance of 150 yards, the length of a football field and a half. (It was eventually replaced by the bow and arrow.)

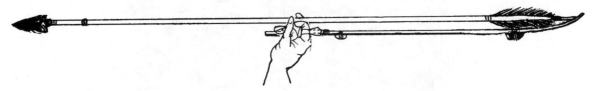

Throwing Stick

Also called the Rabbit Stick, it was used much as a boomerang to bring down small game.

Rabbit Throwing Stick

Nets and Clubs

Rabbit hunts were often a communal activity. A line of walkers held a large woven net as other hunters beat the bushes with short heavy clubs to chase small game into the net where it was killed. Such a net was found in New Mexico in the 1950s. It measured 3 feet high and 100 yards in length. Today, rabbit hunts are held annually each spring at many of the pueblos.

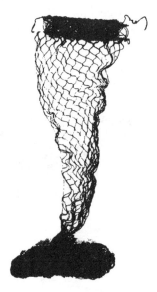

Bow and Arrows

The bow and arrow is a good example of early people working with several natural elements to create a tool. (See Photo 15.) The bow is wood; the bowstring, braided animal hide. The arrow is made of wood, bird feathers, and bird points (arrowheads) of min-

Photo 15. Bow and arrow used in Taos Pueblo. *Courtesy Museum of New Mexico (catalog no. 5030-23-1).*

erals shaped by man. On the shaft of the arrow are two bands of color, one of which is always red, representing danger, death. Lightning designs may appear on the arrow to represent both speed and death. The Jicarilla Apache cut shallow grooves the full length of their arrow shaft. These helped to direct the arrow true to its mark. Called "lightning marks," they served also as blood-letters once the arrow entered its prey.

FOR FARMING

Digging Stick

The Anasazi used a digging stick (about a yard long) for planting. He put his foot on the protruding knob and applied pressure, shoving the stick into the soil and creating a hole where he would then plant seeds. (See Photo 16.) The end of the stick, its point, was hardened by rubbing it with charcoal. This tool was also used for turning over the earth so air and moisture could enter the soil.

Photo 16. Example of a digging stick. *Credit unknown.*

Hoe

The short-handled hoe was made from the shoulder blade of some large animal such as an elk, to which was fastened a sharp piece of stone.

Short handled Hoe made from the shoulder blade of an elk or deer lashed to a stone.

FOR THE HOUSEHOLD

Mano and Metate

Corn grinding was one of the most important duties of the Southwestern Indian woman. The corn was ground between two stones: a stationary one that had a 40-degree angle, the *metate* (meh-tahí-tay): from the Aztec "metatly" meaning grinding slab, and a movable oval stone held in the hands, the *mano* (mah´-no: "hand" in Spanish).

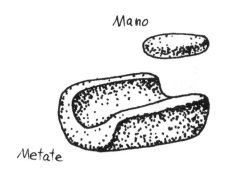

Each home had several metates, some for grinding fine flour and some for coarse flour. First, the corn was dried, then cracked, swept up with a grass brush, and ground again and again until it had a medium-fine texture. Then it was roasted, returned to the metate, and ground again. At this point, the flour was put through a sifting basket and, if desired, reground once more to obtain a very fine flour.

The mano and metate were prized possessions, passed down in a family from mother to daughter.

Today in the Southwest you can see groups of permanent metates formed in rocks on mesa tops where early native women may have ground corn together as they looked out across the vista.

Duma

The *duma* (doó-mah) was the stone on which piki bread was cooked. It was made of sandstone ground smooth with gravel, polished with cottonseed oil, and seasoned with sap from the piñon tree. Finally, the surface was covered with ground melon seed so that the seeds' oil would sink into the stone, turning its surface shiny black. (See Photo 17.) Now the duma was ready to have the cornmeal gruel applied and it would not stick to the stone. A duma was a prized possession to be given to one's daughter when she married.

Fire Drill

This tool uses the principle of rubbing wood on wood to start a fire. The shaft was spun against another piece of wood to create the friction necessary to ignite the wood powder.

Photo 17. Hopi piki maker; circa 1915. *Courtesy Museum of New Mexico (no. CAS 5).*

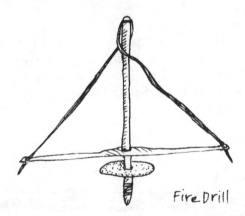

Fire Drill

Cooking Basket

Closely woven baskets were waterproofed with a coating of tree pitch or plant sap. Then instead of heating the outside of their cooking vessel, as we do, the Mogollon dropped clean hot stones into the stew-filled basket and waited for the stones to cook their evening meal.

Coiled Basket
coated with clay to
cook corn with live coals.

Scrapers

Made from deer bone, these hand tools were used for preparing hides for tanning. Bone knives were also common among the Hohokam.

In Pueblo Bonito at Chaco Canyon, New Mexico, in an otherwise empty room in the huge apartment buildings, archaeologists found three such scrapers—each beautifully inlaid with turquoise, shell and jet—and dating back to A.D. 1100.

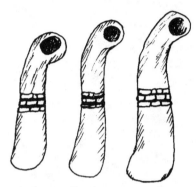

Deer bone Scrapers
inlaid with turquoise, jet, shell
left behind in a room at Pueblo
Bonito.

Hand Axes

These stone axes were used for cutting firewood for the household. At first, axe heads were chipped and notched. In time, full grooved axe heads were developed. Later, oblique (slanted) notches and spiral grooves, also on the oblique, were used for hafting the handle to the improved axe head. Stone hammers were also commonly used by the Mogollon and the Hohokam.

Hand Axe

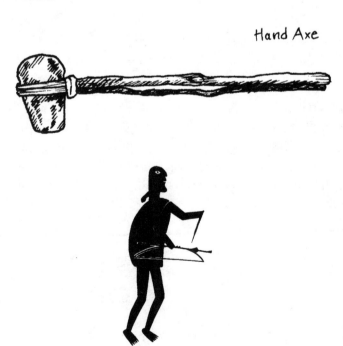

FOR CRAFT-MAKING

Hand Drill

To use this tool you press against the crosspiece, which forces the point of the shank into the material to be drilled and quickly unwinds the leather strip which spins the shank. (The clay disk in the middle acts as a fly wheel; it adds weight and helps keep the shank spinning until the leather strip twists in the opposite direction and raises the crosspiece back to its upper position.) The jeweler then pulls down on the crosspiece again so that the spinning action is repeated in a reverse direction. By rhythmically pumping the crosspiece up and down, a high speed of spinning is achieved and the bit bores cleanly into the piece of turquoise. (See Photo 18.)

Photo 18. Turquoise driller, Zuni Dick; Zuni Pueblo; circa 1930. *Photo by J.R. Willis. Courtesy Museum of New Mexico (neg. no. 108581).*

This pump drill was used to make holes in small pieces of jet, shell, turquoise, or pipestone so that these pieces could be strung (for grinding into bead shapes) to become a necklace. Single flat pieces of turquoise were also drilled to be made into earrings or pendants.

LANGUAGE

Over a thousand distinct languages were spoken in pre-Columbian North America. This gives an indication of the extraordinary diversity of the early American Indian cultures!

NATIVE LANGUAGES OF THE PUEBLOS

Although they have traded and shared many things, the Pueblo people have never shared a common language.

The largest language group among the Pueblos is the *Tanoan* (Tah-noh´-un) which has three main languages: Tiwa (Tee´-wah), Tewa (Tay´-wah), and Towa (Toh´-wah). The Tiwa language is spoken by the people of Taos, Isleta, Picuris, and Sandia Pueblos. Tewa is spoken at Santa Clara, San Juan, San Ildefonso, Nambe, Tesuque, and Pojoaque Pueblos. Towa is spoken at only one pueblo today, at Jemez.

Keresan (Kair´-eh-sahn) is the language spoken in seven pueblos: Santo Domingo, Cochiti, San Felipe, Santa Ana, Zia, Laguna, and Acoma.

The Hopi in north central Arizona speak Hopi (Hoh´-pee), which is related to Pima, Ute and Paiute languages of the Southwest and to several language groups of central Mexico.

The Zunis, who live south of Gallup in New Mexico, speak Zuni(Zoo´-nee), which is not closely related to any other language spoken in the Southwest.

These language differences have helped keep the various pueblos separate from one another. Even people from different pueblos who speak the same language may have trouble understanding one another. Each pueblo group has always thought of itself as independent of, distinct from, every other group. Language differences emphasized this. Five hundred years ago the same was true.

Some Basic Keresan

(as spoken at Cochiti, San Felipe, Santo Domingo, Santa Ana, Laguna, Zia, and Acoma pueblos)

One: *Eeshk*

Two: *Dyoomee*

Three: *Chahm*

Four: *Dyah´neh*

Five: *Tah´m*

Six: *Tchee´zah*

Seven: *My´-yahnah*

Eight: *Coo-coom-shah*

Nine: *Mah´yahk*

Ten: *Kah´ts*

Hello. *Coo waht seenah.*

_____ **is my name.** _____ *eh ehsah.*

I like it. *Skoo-shaw.*

It's beautiful. *Cah-ah uh goomenseh.*

Goodbye. *Doo´ wehshitsah´.*

THE LANGUAGE OF NOMADIC PEOPLES

In about A.D. 825, groups of wandering people from west Canada and Alaska came down to the very edges of the Pueblo world. The Pueblo people called them *Apache*, "the enemy." These nomads spoke the singsong Athabaskan language of the Northwest.

Two hundred years later a second group of wanderers from Canada came to the Southwest and settled largely in northeastern Arizona and northwestern New Mexico. They also spoke Athabaskan and they learned farming from the Pueblos, who called them *Apaches-d´nabuhu´*—"of the big cultivated fields." By the 1600s, these people were called *Navajos* by the Spanish and Pueblo peoples. Today, the Navajo refer to *themselves* as *Dineh* (Dee´-ney), "the people."

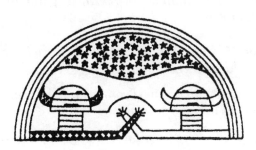

Some Basic Navajo

One: *Tiah-ee*   **Six**: *Hsu-tah*

Two: *Nah-kee*   **Seven**: *Soos-tsle*

Three: *Tanh*   **Eight**: *Tsai-pee*

Four: *Tee*   **Nine**: *Nastai*

Five: *Es-t´lah*   **Ten**: *Nez-nah*

Day: *Chee go*   **Morning star**: *So´tso*

Friend: *Kwa´ssini*   **Sky**: *Ee-yah*

Joy: *Il hozho*   **Sun**: *Cho-ko-no-i*

THE INFLUENCE OF NATIVE LANGUAGES ON ENGLISH

The Native Americans of the eastern coast of North America have contributed a large number of words to the English language, including raccoon, toboggan, moose, caribou, moccasins, and Massachusetts.

In the Southwest, the speaking of native languages was discouraged, first by the Spanish Conquistadors and then by the English-speaking settlers. For this reason, there are very few native words in the spoken language of that region today. Here are four that do appear:

The word *Arizona* comes from the Papago words *ali* meaning "small" and *shonak* meaning "place of the spring." Over the years it gradually changed to have a more Spanish-like sound.

Texas comes from the Caddo people's greeting, *Taysha*, meaning "friend."

Oklahoma means "The Red People" in Choctaw and was first applied to the Indian Territory in 1866.

Utah gets its name from the Ute Indian tribe.

SOUTHWEST NATIVE AMERICAN RIDDLES

The Native people of the Southwest have always enjoyed lighthearted good humor, as the Coyote stories (see the tales later in this section) and the antics of the Koshare and Mudheads (see **Religion and Beliefs**) make clear.

When the people of a culture create riddles, they are playing and having fun with their language. Here are a few examples of Southwest Indian Riddles,[1] some of which date back to the 16th Century!

> *"What is it; what is it? A blue cloth sewn with kernels of popped corn?"*
> **(the night sky and the stars)**

> *"What is it; what is it? A mirror in a room made of pine branches?"*
> **(the eye and eyelashes)**

> *"What is it; what is it? It comes up the valley clapping and clapping like a happy child?"* **(a butterfly)**

> *"Over a flat rock comes a white gourd. What is it?"* **(the moon rising)**

POEMS OF THE SOUTHWEST NATIVE AMERICANS[2]

A poem speaks of ideas and emotions in a more powerful, a more touching, way than ordinary speech. Native American poetry is strong, spare, insightful, and filled with an appreciation for being alive.

The Grey quails were bunched together;
Coyote ran to look upon them.
The Blue quails were bunched together;
Coyote looked sidewise at them.

—**Pima**[3]

The Eagle

The sun's rays
Lie along my wings
And stretch beyond their tips.

—**Papago**[4]

By the sandy water I breathe the odor of the sea,
From there the wind comes and blows over the world.
By the sandy water I breathe the odor of the sea,
From there the clouds come and the rain falls
over the world.

—**Papago**[5]

The magpie! The magpie! Here underneath
In the white of his wings are the footsteps of morning.
It dawns! It dawns!

—**Tewa**[6]

NATIVE AMERICAN STORYTELLING

Storytelling was done seasonally. Tales were not told—nor are they told today—before the first killing frost nor after the first thunders of spring. Stories were told during the inactive (non-farming) months. This kept life in balance.

During the long winter months, early Southwestern people would entertain one another with tales; the elders would instruct the children by retelling stories they had heard from their grandparents. These stories were spiritual reminders and often taught important values: bravery, generosity, honesty, and respect for the old.

"To be a human being in this world today, you gotta hear a lot of stories."

—**Pueblo Indian, 1993**

At the end of a Pueblo Indian story, the elder will say, "What may be learned from this?" It is not a matter of specific answers; rather it allows the listeners to investigate

their responses to the new ideas they have just heard. Why not try using this phrase at the end of each tale you tell in the classroom?[7]

"In Tribal American oral tradition, storytelling is more than simply entertainment—it is a responsible act. To hear a story is to be given the chance to learn to listen carefully—through this, to understand and (be able to) use the stories so you can become a richer and more <u>human</u> being."

—Tom Heidlebaugh, Laughing Bear

Six Native American Tales of the Southwest

Here are six folktales to share with your students.

How Coyote Started It All   (ISLETA PUEBLO)

Welcome all my friends and relations! I want to tell you about how it was in the beginning of all things!

When the animals first came up from the dark onto this earth where we live today, Thought Woman entrusted Coyote with a leather pouch.

"Take this to the new world, Coyote, and do not look inside or it will go hard for you!"

"O.K.," said Coyote.

He took the bag and began to run south. He ran without stopping through many pitch-black nights. But at last his curiosity was just too strong. Coyote stopped and untied the thongs on the leather bag. The second he did, a shower of flashing lights flew out of the pouch and soared up into the sky!

"Now you've done it," hissed Thought Woman. "You couldn't mind your own business, could you? You had to stick your nose where it didn't belong! So be it! From this day on everywhere Coyote goes, trouble will follow."

Right there and then Coyote felt his jaw begin to ache. His back tooth was throbbing. Coyote sat down and reared back his head; he let out a long howl of pain. And so he continued all through the night—howling at the thousand stars that now were twinkling overhead.

So it was and so it is: Coyote's been howling <u>every</u> night since the beginning of this world.

Changing Woman (NAVAJO)

In the time before time began there was only First Man and First Woman. After awhile they heard crying up in the mountains. They went toward the sound and they found a baby girl whose father and mother were Dawn and Darkness.

They took the tiny child down off the mountain and she grew up completely in just 12 days: now she was Changing Woman—the Holy One who is always kind to humans.

She became the bride of the Sun and soon, the mother of twin boys, Monster Slayer and Born for Water.

Then Changing Woman made male corn and female corn and from these she created the first Navajo people.

As the two boys grew—the Hero Twins, as the Navajo call them—they destroyed almost all of man's enemies in Dinetah (Navajo land). So it is said that only four enemies were left: Hunger, Old Age, Poverty, and Dirt.

The Basket Dance (SAN JUAN PUEBLO)

Ha´maha!* There was a San Juan Pueblo boy who was a famous basketmaker.

Well, one day he was out cutting young willow twigs for baskets and he got thirsty so he went to a nearby spring. There he saw a beautiful girl with a jar of water on her head. He asked her for some water and she gave him a gourd dipper from which to drink. Who can say how these things happen, but the moment their eyes met they fell in love!

When the young boy asked her to marry him she said, "Oh, yes, I want to, but I must confess one thing: I am under a spell that sometimes changes me into a water snake called Abanu."

Then the girl took the basketmaker home to meet her grandparents. The old couple was pleased to give them their blessings. So it was that shortly after the boy and girl were married.

Time passed. The newlyweds were very happy and then came the dreadful day when the basketmaker returned home from some travels and he found his wife changed into a long green snake! You can imagine how he felt! He placed the snake to rest in his most beautiful basket and put this on the window ledge so the sun's rays would warm it.

The next morning when he got up, the basketmaker was amazed to find swarms of tiny snakes crawling all over his house! He went to the basket on the ledge and said, "Oh, my wife, oh, Abanu, the snake, what is happening here?"

"These are your babies and you must learn to bear it!" said the serpent. And so the young man did for many a day.

---

*(Hah´-mah-ha!) "In the beginning" or "You must always start from the beginning." This is a very common way for Pueblo stories to be started.

Then, at last, on returning one night from gathering plants for dyes, he was met by his beautiful wife! She had collected all the snakes into four separate baskets and she told him that in order to break the spell, the little snakes had to be driven to the four corners of the Earth—to the East, North, South, and West. She handed him the first group: "Take this first basket toward the sunrise and drive the snakes to the East." This he did.

The second day she said, "Drive these snakes to the North!" And he did it.

On the third day she gave him the third basket and said, "Drive these snakes to the South." And he did as he was told.

Finally on the fourth day she said, "Take this fourth basket toward the sunset and drive these snakes to the West." When the basketmaker did this, the spell was broken and he went to the Pueblo Council and asked it to give a special dance in honor of his wife.

So it was that the Basket Dance was danced for the basketmaker and his beautiful wife. Whenever the dancers brushed the ground with the small branches they carried, they did this to show the trails of the little snakes moving to the East, the North, the South, and the West.

And so it is today that every time the Pueblo Indians dance the Basket Dance, they are retelling the story of the Basketmaker and his bride—and they are honoring the life which they came to have together . . . and that's the end of that story!

Coyote and Horny Toad   (NAVAJO)

One spring Horny Toad was plantin' his garden. He was usin' his diggin' stick. He got the ground all ready and he planted his seeds.

Coyote saw him an' jus' like always he was curious so Coyote come over an' he said, "Watcha doin'?" and 'cause Horny Toad didn't like Coyote, he didn't answer; he jus' kep' on plantin'.

This made Coyote MAD! An' he yelled at Horny Toad, "I said, 'Whatcha doin'?" but Horny Toad pretended he didn' hear Coyote and he jus' kept on diggin' an' plantin'.

Well, this really riled up Coyote and he *really* got mad! "You better answer me or I'll eat you UP, Horny Toad! I said, 'Whatcha doin'?" and 'cause Horny Toad was stubborn he didn't say anythin'. Coyote ate ol' Horny Toad—Gulp!—in one bite!

Once he'd swallowed Horny Toad, Coyote felt him movin' aroun' in there and he said, "Whatcha doin'in there, Horny Toad?"

"I'm lookin' aroun' and it's pink and wrinkly and it's full of mashed berries and ol' dead grasshoppers in here. . . . "

"That's my breakfast! Leave it alone or you'll make me throw up!"

Horny Toad scurried on. . . .

"Whatcha doin' NOW?" Coyote yelped.

"Oh, there's this shiny big ol' red rock in here and I'm lookin' at it!"

"That's my **LIVER**, Horny Toad! You leave that alone! I can't **LIVE** without my liver!"

Horny Toad moved on . . . and Coyote felt those spikes scratchin' his insides and he yelled, "Be careful, Horny Toad! Come on out of there before you hurt me!"

But Horny Toad jus' kep' movin' and so Coyote said, "Hey, whatcha doin' **NOW?**"

"I'm lookin' at this big red fist and it keeps on punchin' back and forth. . . . "

"Yi-yi-ii-i! That's my heart! You leave it alone. You get up out of there, Horny Toad, **RIGHT NOW!**"

But Horny Toad was mad at ol' Coyote for swallowin' him, so he jus' reared back and punched Coyote's heart and that's all it took. . . . Coyote jus' keeled over and laid on the ground not movin' any more.

Horny Toad come on up out of Coyote's throat and he jus' went back to his plantin'. . . .

Now some people say that was the end of Coyote. But other people say that Coyote keeps his livin' secrets in some other place—not in his heart—and so after a long while Coyote got up again, all wobbly and he kinda staggered off into the hills and 'tho Coyote will eat grasshoppers, juniper berries and a mouse when he can get one—ol' Coyote has **NEVER** swallowed a horny toad again since that day.

Now that's a true story—and if it's not, it should be!

The Origin of the Hopi Snake Dance   (*HOPI*)

Once upon a time in the Old People's time, the rains did not fall. The crops at Hopi all turned yellow. The people cried for rain but it did not come. The Hopi people began to die.

One young man named Tiyo (Tee´-yoh) saw the suffering and he said, "I will do something to save my people. I will go and find the Rain."

The Hopis told him, "No one has ever been able to find where Rain lives. Don't go, Tiyo! You'll never come back."

But Tiyo's mind was set. "Rain must live on the other side of the Red Mountains. I will find Rain and I will ask him to come again to Hopi, for if he does not, we will all die."

So Tiyo set out. It took him many days to reach the Red Mountains and many many more to climb to their top. When he had, he looked down and he saw far below in a deep canyon the Big Water and he knew that Rain must live down there too.

Tiyo climbed down into the canyon. He saw how fast the Big Water was running! Tiyo knew what he had to do. He took a fallen log and made it into a boat; then he got into it and shoved it into the Big Water. Off he flew!

All day and night Tiyo roared down the canyon until at last, just at daybreak, the waters slowed and his boat brought him to shore. There he was met by a big tall woman dressed all in black.

"I am Spider Woman and I am going to help you, Tiyo, because I see how *you* do what *must* be done!" Then Spider Woman made magic. She turned herself into a tiny spider and she sat behind Tiyo's right ear.

"Come, Tiyo, I will take you to the Snake People who always know how to get Rain." So off they went.

After many days they reached the Country of the Snake People. Spider Woman told Tiyo, "The Snake People live below the ground in a sacred place called a kiva. You must go down there. I'll wait here for you to come back out."

So Tiyo walked across the kiva roof and climbed down into the kiva. Many many snakes met him inside at the foot of the ladder.

The Snake People liked Tiyo. Because they trusted him, they took off their snake skins and he saw they were really people like you and I.

Tiyo told the Snake People about his search.

"We keep Rain under the ground and, when we make magic, Rain always does as we say." Then the Snake People told Tiyo how to make the magic.

"Your people must sing many songs. The dancers must paint half their bodies white for the clouds and half their bodies black for the rain clouds. They must go out, catch snakes and put sacred cornmeal on them, and then bring them back to Hopi. Then they must dance with the snakes and talk to them and when you let them go, the snakes will all come back here to our kiva and tell us everything. When you do all this, Tiyo, Rain will come to Hopi again!"

Tiyo thanked the Snake People and he returned to Spider Woman. She showed him the way back to his village.

Tiyo told his people everything. The Hopis did all that the Snake People had said to do and Rain returned to Hopi.

So it is that Hopis always remember what Tiyo told them. And whenever they do the right things in the right way, they know the Snake People will bring rain to Hopi once more.

The Well-Baked People   (PIMA)

Once when the world was not as it is today, the Magician had finished making the world. He had completed all the animals. But still something felt not quite . . . right. And then he realized what it was: there should be a creature more like himself on this new earth! So he built an 'orno (oven) and he mixed up some clay with water and shaped this into a figure quite like himself. He laid it down on a log and went off to find some fire-wood.

While the Magician was gone, Coyote came by and quickly changed the clay figure.

The Magician returned with the wood, built a big fire in the 'orno, and heated it up real hot. After he'd brushed out the red coals, he laid the clay figure—without much looking at it, really—onto the floor of the oven.

Time passed and the Magician went to the 'orno to see how his creation was doing. He took it out, breathed Life onto it, and then he looked at it: "Say, this is not the Man

I made to live on the new world! *This* looks like . . . **COYOTE**! . . . Ai-ee-ee! I've been tricked!"

Now Coyote, tail between his legs, came out of the shadows. "Well," he whined, "**I** needed a friend to keep **ME** company in this new world **TOO!**"

"Oh, okay," the Magician said, "but don't you fool with my creations from here on!" . . . and that's how we got the dog. . . .

Now the Magician thought, "If I make just one figure, he'll get lonesome too. I better make one to keep him company." So the Magician took some more clay and made two figures and laid them side by side in the 'orno.

A little time passed and Coyote said, "You'd better take them out now or they'll get over-baked!" So the Magician took them out. He breathed on them and gave them Life—but the Magician looked at the two figures and grumbled, "Coyote, you had me take them out too early. Look at them. They don't belong here in the Southwest. They're all pale! They have to live on the other side of the world," and he sent them off. "Now I'll have to start all over again!"

This time the Magician waited quite a long time before he took the figures out of the 'orno. He brushed the ashes off them and breathed onto them to give them Life. He said, "Now, these are baked to a beautiful brown! These are just right to live here in the Southwest!"

The new man and the new woman laughed and walked around and held hands and were glad.

The Magician—who was now Man and Woman Maker—looked at his last creation and he smiled.

"All-RIGHT! *These* are perfect."

And that's how we got the first Pima people!

Notes for "Language":

1. This is a random collection of old Southwestern Indian riddles. Other Native American riddles can be found in *Make Prayers to the Raven* by Richard Nelson.

2. From *Song of the Pima.* Reprinted by permission of the Smithsonian Institution.

3. From *Singing for Power* by Ruth Underhill. Reprinted with permission of the University of California Press.

4. From Bureau of American Ethnology Bulletin No. 90 (1929). Appeared in "Papago Music" by Francis Densmore. Reprinted by permission of the Smithsonian Institution.

5. From "Navajo Gambling Songs" by Washington Matthews which appeared in *American Anthropologist* (vol. 2, no. 1). Reprinted with permission of the publisher.

6. Stories strengthen the listener and help the boy or girl become a man or woman. Stories told today through the media are mainly observed and can never take the place of tales told by elders, which offer wisdom shared by another human being. Sometimes teachers who are not of Native American heritage feel uncomfortable with the idea of telling Native American tales. Certainly whenever Native American storytellers, themselves, are available to come into your classroom, this is the experience you would offer your students. However, it is more important that the child hear these ancient tales than whether the storyteller has Native American ancestors.

"Bringing a story to life is the art of storytelling and that journey transcends any cultured boundaries."

—Lloyd Arneach, Cherokee historian and storyteller

ARTS AND CRAFTS

There is no word for "art" in either the Navajo or Pueblo languages. These native people see creativity, beauty, and skill as being basic to every part of life.

For the Navajos, beauty is more than pleasing colors, shapes, or lines. It is harmony in nature, a sense of security in your community, and physical and emotional well-being in each of us.

In Beauty I Walk[1]

With beauty before me, I walk.
With beauty behind me, I walk.
With beauty above me, I walk.
With beauty all around me, I walk.
With beauty within me, I walk.
It is finished in beauty.

—Navajo

Once the necessities of life are taken care of, people think of creating adornments and objects of beauty.

"These things that we make—these and the land—are (given to us) to help us know ourselves—and to help answer 'Where am I going?'"

—Pearl Sunrise, Navajo weaver, 1992

BASKETRY

The first Southwestern baskets were made 10,000 years ago. From the beginning, baskets were an essential tool for survival as they were the basic containers—long before pottery was created. Woven from grasses, reeds, willow, yucca, sumac, and vegetable fibers, they were used to carry objects, or store grains and seeds. Most baskets were lightweight and strong. When caulked with resin, a basket held water; when hot stones were added, these baskets became cooking vessels. Basket work was not simply involved with the making of receptacles. Basketry also produced fences, houses, robes, shoes, cradles, and finally, burial objects. (See Photo 19.)

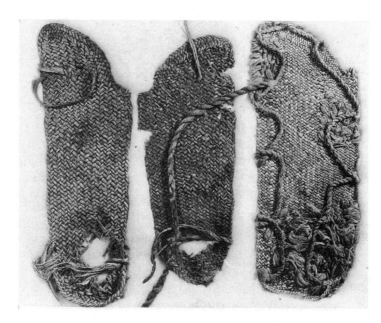

Photo 19. Pre-Columbian woven sandals made of yucca leaf, a.d. 1000-2000; circa 1940. *Photo by Wyatt Davis. Courtesy Museum of New Mexico (neg. no. 43934).*

Of all the Native American basketmakers, the Apache were historically the most extraordinary. The Papago and Hopi also are known for their outstanding baskets.

Wicker Baskets

These baskets were made by first laying down, side by side, a group of sumac twigs. A second group of such twigs was laid at a right angle over the first group. The weaver then took flexible lengths of rabbit brush (a desert plant) and wove these over and under the overlapping sumac twigs. (See Photo 20.)

Photo 20. Unidentified basket maker of San Ildefonso Pueblo; circa 1900. *Courtesy Museum of New Mexico (neg. no 42328).*

Shallow Baskets and Trays

These were formed by wrapping thin yucca leaves around the stems of Hilaria grass to form a smooth coil. Yucca strands were finally used to sew the concentric coils together. (See Photo 21.)

Photo 21. Pima (?) basket. *Courtesy Museum of New Mexico (neg. no. 21835).*

Burden Baskets

The Apache women wove the burden basket with its decorative leather thongs. Today, the leather thongs are capped with little metal tinklers. The Mescalero Apaches are currently involved with restoring their basket arts.

Photo 22A is an example of an Ácoma burden basket. Photo 22B shows a Pima woman in 1935 wearing a burden basket.

Photo 22A. Burden basket; Ácoma Pueblo. *Photo by Arthur Taylor. Courtesy Museum of New Mexico (neg. no. 74214).*

Photo 22B. Pima woman with kiho or burden basket; circa 1935. *Photo by Frasher. Courtesy Museum of New Mexico (neg. no. 74986).*

Wedding Baskets

Made of sweet-smelling sumac, these baskets are woven by Navajos and Paiutes. The colors used are creamy white, reddish brown, and black. The white center represents the underworld; the jagged black, the mountains and valleys of the upper world; while the reddish band stands for the *sipapu* (see-pah-poo´), the path of emergence that traditionally was taken when the first people came up to this world. The Paiutes believe that if this band of red were closed, no more children would be born into this upper world. The Navajos believe that this band was an escape path for any evil spirits. The basket ends in a braided stitch directly opposite the sipapu opening; this must always be facing east (in honor of the sun) whenever the basket is held.

This basket is used to hold sacred cornmeal during religious ceremonies and during the traditional part of a Pueblo or Navajo wedding.

Papago Baskets

Papago women split bear grass for the foundation of their baskets, which were often pale yellow with a creamy-colored over-stitching The basket shapes vary from flattened bowl shape to the tall, straight-sided storage baskets. (See Photo 23.)

Photo 23. Papogo coiled basket bowl; yucca; 7-1/8″ diameter, 1-5/8″ high; 1965. *Photo by Arthur Taylor. Courtesy Museum of New Mexico (neg. no 98593).*

Pima Baskets

A few Pima women are continuing the Pima basket-making tradition.[2]

In a society where life and religion are one, Native American baskets are holy symbols as well as practical objects. Used at shrines, in rituals, a basket filled with holy images would be lifted overhead to better carry the people's prayers to the spirits above.

Basketry leads very naturally into pottery-making and weaving on the loom!

Early Pima Basket Design

POTTERY

More settled living conditions allowed for and encouraged pottery-making. Pots can hold, store, and be used for cooking food directly over the fire. For these reasons, pots gradually replaced baskets, which are actually practical for people on the move.

The first Southwestern pottery, made by the Mogollon people, was created almost 2,000 years ago. The Mogollon learned from their Mexican neighbors how to mold and fire clay containers.

In time, the Anasazi influenced the Mogollons' pottery-making. This is first seen in the addition of geometric designs to the surface of their pots and eventually by the use of extraordinary black-on-white paintings of abstracted animals and people on the Mimbres pottery.

How Early Southwestern Pottery Was Probably Made

1. The (hard, crumbly) clay was dug out of traditional clay pits. It was crushed and sifted.

2. Next, it was soaked in water until it was of a good consistency. (Today, some Pueblo potters mix their clay at this point with ground prehistoric pot fragments, or shards, to give the clay added strength.)

3. The potter flattened out a lump of clay between her hands to form a base. She rolled a long coil of clay and joined it to the outer edge of the base and continued to wind the coils atop one another to form a wall. She smoothed and molded the pot between her fingers by using a flat stick. She let the pot dry a bit and then used a curved piece of dried gourd to gently scrape the pot's walls to make them uniform. (See Photo 24.)

Photo 24. Ana (left), Maria Martinez (second from left), not identified, and Ramona (right) making pottery on placita (patio) of Palace of the Governors in Santa Fe, New Mexico; circa 1912. *Courtesy Museum of New Mexico (no. 22947).*

4. A coat of slip—white clay and water—was applied and when it was dry, it was rubbed with a smooth stone to make it shine.

5. Next, the potter chewed a piece of yucca spear to soften the fibers—forming a thin brush. She dipped this brush into clay paint to draw a design on her pot. (See Photo 25.)

Photo 25. Julian and Maria Martinez of San Ildefonso Pueblo making pottery on patio of Palace of the Governers in Santa Fe, New Mexico; circa 1912. *Photo by Jesse L. Nusbaum. Courtesy Museum of New Mexico (neg. no 40814).*

6. After drying several days, the pot was fired in a pile of smoldering dung because this material burns with an even heat. (See Photo 26.)

Photo 26. A firing mound in San Ildefonso Pueblo. *Courtesy Museum of New Mexico (no. 41587).*

Early Southwestern pottery forms included both practical and sacred containers and freestanding animals as well as human figures.

For centuries, the main reason for the designs on Southwestern pottery was the making of "picture prayers" asking for rain, fertility, and good hunting. For this reason, the designs included clouds, lightning, rain, mountains (where rain is seen falling), polliwogs and frogs (both water creatures), seed pods, leaves (symbolizing good crops), and birds and feathers (to carry prayers upward).

Because it was the inner spirit of the bird or animal or force of Nature that the artist was attempting to capture, a physically accurate portrayal was not necessary. The spiritual feel of the creature was what the artist sought.

We can only imagine the specific meaning of the figures of the designs on the pottery. But based on interviews with potters in the early 19th Century, it is believed that these figures, and certain vessels—as with the ceremonies and dances—were made to help keep a balance between the world of humans, and nature, and the world of the spirit. (See Photo 27.)

Photo 27. Hopi bowl by Nampeyo; circa 1890-1910. *Photo by Arthur Taylor. Courtesy Nuseum of New Mexico (neg. no. 68434).*

Pueblo religion is present in all of daily life. Shaping a pot is a sacred activity.

"So I'll be sure to get a perfect clay, I go with prayer (corn) meal. I go to a shrine there and ask for permission to take clay and (ask) for health, happiness, peace in the world. I breathe into the (corn) meal and exhale into the universe. I put the clay through two screenings (to sift out impurities) and then through the leg of a pantyhose. Before I shape it, I pray, 'Mother, Father, Spirits gone before me: It is me, your daughter, Shree Si Uai, with prayer and permission I take you, Clay, from your ancient home. With my fingers I mold you (in) to a new creation. With prayer and fire you attain new strength; with your completion you bless me wholly. Accept my offering, please, my Mother, my Father. Thank you.' This is the way it is."

—**Angelina Medina, Ácoma-Zia, contemporary potter**

WEAVING

The Navajos learned how to weave from the Pueblo people who wove cotton, fur, feathers, and string. Once the Spanish brought sheep to the Southwest, the Navajos began to make and weave with woolen yarn.

To make yarn you first sheared the sheep. This raw wool was carded to take out the burrs and to untangle the wool. Next, it was washed in yucca suds and spun on a wooden spindle. The spindle was always turned clockwise as this is the direction in which the sun, itself, always moves. Sometimes the wool would be spun five or six separate times in order to achieve a very refined yarn!

Nearly all the colors in a Navajo rug are taken from plant dyes that must be obtained over a period of an entire year. This is because some dyes are made from a single plant whose roots produce different colors in different seasons! In this way, a Navajo rug represents humans working together with animals, plants, and the cycles of the seasons. (See Photo 28.)

Photo 28. Navajo women weaving, carding, spinning, and tending flock of sheep; circa 1940. *Courtesy Museum of New Mexico (neg. no. 127458).*

Navajo women use a vertical loom and weave out-of-doors. The weaver kneels on the ground and begins her weaving at the bottom of the loom. The vertical threads on the loom are called the warp. She passes the horizontal yarn, the weft, over and under the warp threads (using a little stick, not a shuttle). Then she taps down the weft in that row using a thin wooden stick.

Belts and sashes are woven on simple looms with the warp threads attached to the weaver's own belt and tied to a housepole or a tree.

Many Navajo rugs have a border that is interrupted by a gap at one point. This is the *ch'indibitün*, "road of bad spirits." This is to allow an exit for any negative thoughts on the part of any weaver who might believe that an absolutely perfect design could ever be achieved. If, however, she has already left a small deviation in the pattern, she does not have to leave a gap in the border.

Oh our Mother, the Earth, Oh our Father, the Sky,
Your children are we, and with tired backs
We bring you the gifts that you love.
Then weave for us a garment of brightness.

May the warp be the white light of morning,
May the weft be the red light of evening,
May the fringes be the falling rain,
May the border be the standing rainbow.

Thus weave for us a garment of brightness
That we may walk fittingly where the birds sing,
That we may walk fittingly where grass is green,
Oh our Mother, the Earth, Oh our Father, the Sky.

—Tewa[3]

PREHISTORIC JEWELRY

Bracelets

The Hohokam ground the Glycymeris shell smooth. Next, they sliced the shell, removing the top so that the base became a bracelet. This was re-ground and decoration was added by carving, using inlaid or overlaid mosaic or by etching or painting.

Shell Bracelets

Etching

The Hohokam discovered how to etch shells in about A.D. 900. It involved coating the inside or outside of a Cardium shell with pitch or tree gum. These coated areas would not be etched. The shell was then dipped into the fermented juice of a saguaro cactus. Every uncoated part of the shell would be eaten into by this acid. Once the etching was of the desired depth, the shell was washed off, the pitch or gum removed, and the design was clearly shown. Sometimes mineral painting was added to further decorate the shell.

The Hohokam often used the frog as a design on shells and jewelry. This was because in their desert setting, frogs were associated with rain as they appear there in great numbers after any rainfall.

Etched Shell

Necklaces

Thin pieces of turquoise or shell[4] were ground to the right thickness, then scored and broken into tiny squares, one for each bead. The corners were broken off to form rough circles and each was drilled—the big beads with a stone drill and the small ones with a cactus spine! The beads were then tightly strung and rolled back and forth on a sandstone slab to make them really round.

Archaeologists believe that it took about 15 minutes for a prehistoric jeweler to make one bead. This included collecting the material, constructing the drill, and working the material into a necklace. It would, therefore, have required 30 days of working 8 hours a day for the Hohokam craftsman to have made a 24-inch necklace!

Metal Work

The only metal work done prehistorically in the Southwest was the making of copper bells, which date from A.D. 1000-1400. They were cast by the lost wax process that was learned from Mexican traders.

To make a bell, the craftsman would first make an exact model from wax. This model was put in the middle of a clay ball that had an opening at the top that led down to the bell.

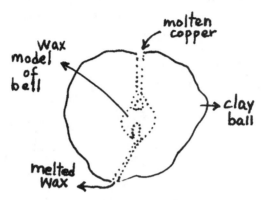

Molten copper was poured into the opening in the clay and this caused the wax to melt and flow out a tiny hole at the bottom of the clay ball. In this way, the hot metal replaced the bell-shaped wax area in the clay. Once the copper had completely cooled, the clay was broken away, revealing the tiny copper bell!

Notes for "Arts and Crafts":

1. "In Beauty I Walk" translation from *Songs of the Tewa* by Herbert J. Spinden.

2. In 1993 I sat next to a Pima woman during a Fourth of August feast at Santo Domingo Pueblo. I asked her about basket-making on her reservation and she replied, "We're learnin' again."

3. "The Sky Loom" is a Tewa Prayer for well being. The Sky Loom refers to small desert rains that resemble a loom hung from the sky. Translation from *Songs of the Tewa* by Herbert J. Spinden.

4. Early necklaces were made of shell, travertine, turquoise, black argillite, and pipestone. Other materials used by prehistoric craftsmen include red argillite dug from hills around Prescott, Arizona and jet that was taken from bituminous coal beds by the Anasazi. Early people also worked the turquoise mines southeast of Santa Fe, New Mexico. The Hohokam used turquoise that they took from various mines including present-day Kingman and Bisbee mines.

CHILDREN AND PLAY

One way to measure the development of a culture is to look at its attitude toward children to see how protective or caring its adults are toward youngsters and to see what kinds of games, toys, and play it encourages during free time. If play is thought of as a preparation for being grown-up, what parts of adulthood did the (Native American) culture emphasize in the games, stories, and toys it provided for its children?

Photo 29. Navajo woman and child at Laguna Pueblo encampment; circa 1935. *Photo by T. Harmon Parkhurst. Courtesy Museum of New Mexico (neg. no. 3239).*

CHILDREN

Early Native American parents were fond of their children, decorating their clothes and cradleboards, forming tiny clay dishes or bows and arrows for their amusement. At the same time, these first Southwestern people were strict parents. Children had plenty of time to play, yet they were expected at an early age to begin helping their families.

Girls babysat the infants and practiced weaving baskets; they gathered wild foods, made pottery, and ground corn.

Boys were taken to the fields to help in the raising of crops; they learned to hunt and to weave cotton.

Discipline was often gained through the use of fear.

Owl Song[1]

Owls, owls, big owls and little,
Staring, glaring, eyeing each other,
Children, from your cradleboards, oh see!
Now the owls are looking at you, looking at you,
Saying, "Any crying child, Yellow Eyes will eat him up."
Saying, "Any naughty child, Yellow Eyes will eat him up."

—**Hopi**

Each group of Native Americans had specific ways of marking a child's life as it passed from youth into adulthood. Here is a description of the Navajo's ritual of this passage. (See also **Social Groups and Government** for a description of the Apache coming-of-age ceremony.)

The Nightway Chant: A Navajo Ritual for Young People

On the last night of this ceremony (See Photo 30), Navajo girls and boys, aged 7 to 13, are initiated into the adult ceremonial life of their people:

The Grandfather of the Monsters and the Female Goddess come forward and lead a child up to the blazing fire. The young boys are naked to the waist. One of the sacred figures places cornmeal on the child's shoulder and the other strikes the boy with a bundle of reeds; both figures cry out in high-pitched voices. Eventually, at the end of the ceremony, the children come to understand these tall creatures. The children return, enlightened, to their families and homes.

PLAY

Toys

Early Southwestern children played with stilts, tops, bows and arrows, bean shooters, targets, sling-shots, dolls, tiny dishes, wicker cradleboards, and buzzmakers.

Photo 30. Dancers from the Navajo "Night Chant." *Credit unknown.*

These were made from natural materials such as wood, clay, bone, seeds, thorns, stones, leather, vines, and feathers.

When Native American children played with their toys, they were often imitating adults (hunting, caring for families), perfecting physical skills (strength, accuracy, speed), or reinforcing religious beliefs (in supernatural beings by playing with kachina dolls or bullroarers).

Puppets

Puppet shows held in the kivas, the underground ceremonial rooms, were performed for both the viewers' amusement as well as their religious instruction.

Kachina "Dolls"

At the Hopi Goyohim Kachina ceremony, some kachina dancers carry figures carved of cottonwood root, each painted and dressed to represent a specific spirit from

Tourist Kachina
Dolls: these non-religious
little figures are carved as souvenirs
of the Southwest.

the nearby mountains. These "dolls" are actually teaching devices given to young girls for instruction in religious legends and symbolism. (Small bows and arrows are given to the young boys.) These kachina figures are to be respected as they represent spirits who bring calm days, good health, and strength to Hopis. These kachina figures are hung from *vigas* (rafters) or the walls where they may be seen and studied at all times.

A flat wooden kachina doll may be tied to a baby's cradleboard where it can be fondled by the infant. These cradle kachinas are simplified versions of the larger dolls.

Often, toys were at first identified with mythic or legendary origins. For example, the ball was thought to have come from the sun and/or the moon and as a sacred object, it was not to be touched by human hands. (During the early ball games, this was always the rule!) The Navajo String Figures were said to have been given to the Navajos by Spider Woman!

Games

Certain early games were a form of spiritual training meant to instill in the player a sense of cooperation with the group as well as a feeling of personal striving for improvement. Children were taught by watching their elders rather than by being coached. You played for the pleasure of the game itself.

"When running, set your sights on the mountain, not on the man in front of you."

**—Steve Guchupin,
champion runner of San Juan Pueblo**

The early native people on the whole believed that when a player won a game or race, or when there was a fortunate occurrence during play, this was actually an expression of encouragement being sent by a supernatural being and, for no reason that the player would understand. ("Bad luck" during a game was seen as the reverse of this.)

Guessing Games

Some Native American players believed that they were gifted with extrasensory perception that permitted them to make correct judgments. Other good players felt they understood how people act when trying to fool or deceive you and this allowed them to make correct guesses. Some players put their faith in the charms they had painted on their gaming sticks, which they believed "caused the sticks to fall as they wanted them to fall"! (For descriptions of specific games, see the **Activities** section.)

Note for "Children and Play":

1. From *In the Trail of the Wind: American Indian Poems and Orations,* edited by John Bierhorst, © 1971 by J. Bierhorst. Reprinted with permission of the author.

Photo 31. Four Kossa Clowns. San Juan, 1935. *Photo by T. Harmon Parkhurst. Courtesy Museum of New Mexico (no. 3895).*

RELIGION AND BELIEFS

Religion is an extremely private subject for most southwestern Native people. For this reason only very general non-sacred information is included below.

RELIGIOUS BELIEFS HELD IN COMMON

Religious practices among the early Native people varied, but certain religious beliefs are shared by all—by the Hopi, Zuni, the Pueblo, and the Navajo peoples.

Be respectful of Nature, of all living things. The earth is sacred, as are water and the air. They are gifts to us, and to all beings, and are for the benefit of all.

Each thing in Nature has a spirit and may be spoken to through ceremonies and rites that the spirits, themselves, set up at the beginning of the world.

All things in the Universe are connected, one to another . . .

" . . . *we are all one, indivisible. Nothing that any of us does but affects us all.*"

—"The Man Who Killed the Deer" by Frank Waters

Try to live in such a way that you may stay in harmony with the Natural World. It is through harmony that each of us remains in good health and through balance that the world, itself, may also continue.

To the Native American, religion, magic, and science are intertwined. Disease is cured by chanting, singing, *and* through the use of herbal remedies; game is acquired by prayer and the use of good hunting skills. The natural and the supernatural work as one.

To the Native American, religion is not a separate part of their lives. It is present at all times, part of all activities. . . . Life is religion.

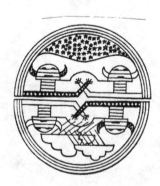

Hunting and farming were basic to the early Pueblo people. Because both of these activities involve chance, the Pueblo people tried to improve their control over fortune by developing rites of magic and religion. Farming made the Pueblo people very conscious of weather. Seasonal rituals quite naturally were created and these became the basis of the Pueblo Indian religion.

CEREMONIAL DANCES

Most Pueblo dances are like little plays and refer to the relationship between people and Nature or people and the Great Spirit. Everything the dancers wear and every move they make is symbolic. The Pueblo Indians believe that participating in dances is an honor[1] and that each dance is a gift of energy and renewal to the participants as well as to the viewers.[2] While many dances at the pueblos are open to the public, these are religious ceremonies, not tourist performances. (Powwows, on the other hand, include dance exhibitions specifically for the pleasure and entertainment of the spectators and tourists.)

Behind the dancers there is a large group of men called the chorus. Their singing accompanies the dancers and their movement is a way of asking the clouds for rain, or speaking to some other parts of Nature. The deep-sounding drum "wakes up the clouds, or other creatures, and cheers up the people."

There are many different types of dances: those that ask for a good harvest or a successful hunt, those that celebrate a new season, or honor a certain part of nature. The animal dances, such as the Buffalo and Deer Dances, are given to help everything in Nature live together in a more harmonious way. The Hopi Snake Dance plays out part of the legend. It involves nine days of ceremonies. Snakes are collected and for eight days are ritually bathed and stroked with eagle feathers by the Antelope and Snake Priests.

The Hopi Snake Dance

This extraordinary dance is performed by the Snake and the Antelope Brotherhoods. A nine-day ceremony, it occurs every other year in late summer and evolves from The Legend of the Hopi Snake Dance (see **Language** chapter.) Its purpose is to offer a plea for rain and a good harvest. (See Photo 32.)

To begin with, live snakes (many of which are rattlesnakes) are captured from each of the four directions and are brought to the Snake Kiva, a sacred underground room. There, the serpents are given ritual baths and are kept awake in pots or on the floor. They are continually stroked by two men with eagle feather whips (two eagle feathers on a short wooden handle). This action soothes the snakes and keeps them from coiling so they cannot strike.

Just before sunset on the ninth day, the Snake and Antelope Priests, and the young boys who are being initiated into the society, come up out of the kiva. The boys' bodies are painted blue or white and the priests have black faces with white chins. They wear feathers or fir branches on their heads and their long hair hangs free. They wear silver bracelets, shell necklaces, cotton kilts, woven belts; each dancer also wears turtle shell clappers on his right knee and has a fox hide hanging down in back. A long line of the Antelope Priests comes first, shaking gourd rattles to sound like raindrops. They circle the plaza four times, the head priest sprinkling cornmeal on the ground, and another priest whirling a bullroarer overhead to symbolize thunder.

Photo 32. Hopi "Snake Dance." *Courtesy Museum of New Mexico (no. CAS 16).*

A *kisi* (kee´-see), an enclosure made of cottonwood branches, stands to one side of the plaza. In front of it on the ground lays a board. This symbolizes the *sipapu* (see-pah-poo´), the place of Emergence from the Underworld into this world. Each priest dances by this board and stamps on it to show the spirit below that "he is here." Then these priests form a single line next to the kisi and face the plaza.

Now the Snake priests enter. Their chests and backs are painted black with white lightning. They have red feathers in their hair and red rings around their eyes. White paint encircles their mouths. They dance around the plaza four times. Then the first Snake Priest goes and crouches in front of the kisi. He takes a live snake out of the sipapu and holds it in his mouth between his teeth. Then he stands up facing the Antelope Priest who puts his arm around the other's shoulder and begins stroking the dangling snake with his feather wand. Staying in step together, the two priests dance with the snake around the plaza. The Hopi women sprinkle sacred cornmeal on them as they pass.

Then the Snake Priest tosses the snake to the ground and a snake catcher picks it up so it can't escape. The two priests return to the kisi for another serpent. (See Photo 33.)

Photo 33. Hopi "Snake Dance." *Courtesy Museum of New Mexico (no. CAS 1).*

These actions are repeated by a long line of pairs of priests. There may be 200 dancers with their 100 snakes in the plaza at one time! Once all the snakes have taken part in the ceremony, they are tossed into the middle of a large ring of cornmeal and sacred cornmeal is sprinkled on them. (See Photo 34.)

Photo 34. Hopi "Snake Dance." *Painting by Hopi artist Fred Kabotie. Courtesy Museum of New Mexico (no. 6951).*

Finally, the priests grab as many snakes as they can with their bare hands and they each run off down the mesa, to the plains below, where they say special prayers and free the snakes who become messengers to the gods. The men return to the mesa top where they cleanse themselves and, that night, enjoy a big feast.

The prayer which the Snake Priests give during the Snake Dance says: *"Send us clouds, lightning, thunder and rain. Then will the corn mature and there will be food for the people. Then will there be joy in the village. The children will play. The young people will laugh and all hearts will be filled with thanksgiving."*

—**quoted by Dowawisima, Hopi**

KACHINAS

The Kachina is the spirit, the invisible force, of any element of the natural world, including spirits of the dead. The origin of the Kachinas lies far back in prehistory. Kachinas were a part of the Anasazi's religious beliefs. Paintings of these sacred messengers are found on prehistoric pottery and kiva walls and, occasionally, a carved kachina is found in an ancient kiva.

The Hopi think of themselves as being directly descended from the Anasazi. They believe that the Kachinas were always with them, even as they came up out of Mother Earth. Kachinas are not gods, but they are the messengers between humans and the gods. Their main task is to bring rain and to ensure a good harvest for the Hopi people.

There are as many as 335 individual Kachinas, each with a specific name, identity, dance, and song. Here are some types of Kachinas:

Chief Kachinas (Mongwikachinum)

These are the wise and powerful representatives of the spirit world. Each Chief looks out for the interests of one clan (or a group of related clans).

Guard Kachinas (Tuwalakum)

When they appear on their own, they are policemen, guarding a ceremony or "enforcing the cleaning of a well." When they appear as a group, they are warriors.

The Ogres (Sosoyok´t)

These are disciplinary Kachinas. A week before the Powamu Ceremony, Ogre Woman goes through the villages of First and Second Mesa. At each house she tells the younger children that the boys must catch mice (with the yucca snares she provides) and the girls must grind corn. In one week she will return to see how they've done—and if she is displeased, she will take the children for food!

A week later she comes back with lots of menacing kachinas who demand meat and corn! The children's mice and corn are rejected and more "food" is required. Then the children's poor behavior of the last weeks is cited and the parents offer other food in place of their children. The Ogres take the food and leave. Later, the village men lure the Ogres into a dance and then take back the ill-gotten food! The Ogres are made to leave the village empty-handed.

The children learn three important lessons from all this: They must contribute to the food supply or die. Their safety depends on the good will of their family. And village men will finally protect the people of Hopi.

Kachina Women (Momoyam)

They are the sisters, wives and mothers of the male kachinas. (In dances, all the women kachinas but one, Pachaviun Mana, are played by men who freely choose these roles.)

Mixed Kachinas (Sosoyohim Katchinum)

All of these—whether insect, cloud or other spirit—are meant to bring rain. These kachinas are drawn to gaiety and for this reason many dances are meant to attract them as they will bring rain.

Indian Kachinas (Sosoyohim Ustam Katchinum)

These figures represent neighboring tribes—not the physical likenesses, but the essence of the people. They play many ceremonial roles, often as "uncles" in mixed dances.

Runner Kachinas (Wawash Kachinum)

In spring, they challenge village men to race. If a man should lose, the Kachina will punish him, e.g., by stripping him in public. If the man wins, he is often given piki bread. These races may be just for fun or, as some say, the kachinas may reward village participation by sending rain.

Clowns (Chuchkut)

The Mudheads make fun of the most serious people and subjects. No one is safe from the barbs of these anti-clowns.

At winter solstice the Hopi men hold a ceremony asking the sun to return so their crops will grow. This is when the Kachinas appear and they stay with the Hopi until the summer solstice when they return to their homes in the mountains.

Long ago the actual Kachina beings came yearly and showed the Hopi how to hunt, how to fish, and how to bring rain. After eons, the Kachinas stopped coming and another way was needed to contact the gods. Each year in sacred ceremonies the representatives of those first Kachinas return to the villages and bring hope and energy once more to the people.

MEDICINE MEN AND MEDICINE WOMEN

All groups of Native Americans have medicine women and/or medicine men. Native American medicine may involve healing, forecasting good and evil, protecting against attack, or strengthening a person. Medicine people are believed to be born with special talents that are their personal "medicine." They also receive traditional curing knowledge from the elders.

There are two kinds of Southwestern Native American medicine: natural and intuitive. These may be used separately or together. The *natural* includes use of plants (bark, roots, twigs, leaves) and animals (e.g., the Apache use spider eggs; the Papago use crickets; the Navajo applies the ashes of a centipede to the centipede bite on the patient!). *Intuitive* medicine involves the power to know at once, to understand without conscious reasoning. This type of medicine is a natural gift.

The Navajos believe that an illness occurs when a person is out of harmony with Nature. The medicine person may cure the illness by using song, chants, dance, prayer, sand painting, and/or medicinal plants.

The Zia Pueblo people believe that medicine workers get their power to heal from supernatural animals and that the power to heal is found in fetishes.

THE FETISH OR ANIMAL HELPER

The fetish is an object believed to have magical powers; it is an animal helper or guardian.

The first fetishes were pieces of mineral that naturally looked like animals or people. Early Zunis called these *Ahlashine*, "stone ancients," and believed they were the actual people or animals somehow turned to stone and that they carried the powers of the ancients.

Thousand-year-old fetish necklaces have been discovered on which tiny fetish birds and animals carved from turquoise, sandstone, serpentine, or shell have been included. These little fetishes were roughly picked out of the mineral with a sharp, hard stone and the figure was then polished smooth with sand.

All Southwest Native people have made fetishes.[3] The Zunis, however, are the most renowned and they sometimes supplied fetishes to the other Southwest tribes.

A fetish may be made of mineral, bone, beaded leather, or lizard skin. The area in which a person lived dictated the material(s) used.

A personal fetish could be obtained in any of several ways: from a dream, a slain enemy, or as a found object, but its exact origin would be kept a secret. The owner had to believe that the fetish had some symbolic connection with the power of the universe. The owner would also be respectful, prayerful, and keep the fetish supplied with small amounts of sacred cornmeal.

A fetish does not represent an animal spirit, it *embodies* that spirit. They are used to draw into oneself the power of the animal involved. The Zunis believe that fetishes bring success in hunting and farming or provide good fortune.

SAND PAINTINGS

These dry sand designs are said by the Navajo to represent ancient paintings done on the clouds by the *Yei* (yay), or gods. Navajos long ago got the sand-painting technique from the Pueblos, but the images they use are from their own myths.

Traditionally, Navajo sand paintings have been made on the floor of a hogan when a medicine man conducted a religious ceremony to bring safety, beauty or rain, or to cure an illness. This Singer, as he is called, is a respected learned man who has memorized hundreds of sand paintings—each with a different power—each to honor or beg help from the *Yei*, the Holy Ones who look after the people.

Working smoothly and precisely, the medicine man lets the dry pigments (colored sand, pollen, charcoal, cornmeal or ground minerals) sift down between his thumb and the notch at the first joint of his forefinger. The completed painting may be up to 12 feet square. (See Photos 35A and 35B.)

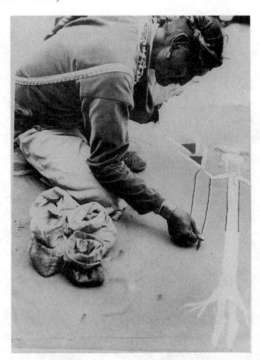

Photo 35A. Navajo sand painter; circa 1935. *Courtesy Museum of New Mexico (neg. no. 8718).*

Photo 35B. Navajo sand painting at Gallup Indian ceremonial in Gallup, New Mexico. *Photo by Wyatt Davis. Courtesy Museum of New Mexico (neg. no. 44175).*

The patient sits, or is laid, in the middle of the finished painting in order to absorb the powers shown in it and to let any evil in his or her body drain down into the fine sand.

At the end of a rite, the medicine man takes colored sands from several parts of the *Yei* in the painting and applies them to the sick person's body. (See Photo 36.) When the sick person is cured, he or she is restored to perfect harmony with nature.

Photo 36. Boy seated upon sand painting. *Courtesy Museum of Navajo Ceremonial Art.*

A sand painting begun after sunrise must be destroyed before sunset and one made after sundown must be destroyed before sunrise. Once the ritual is over, the medicine man erases the painting in a specific way.[4]

RITES OF DEATH

There is not much evidence concerning prehistoric religious ceremonies, but a few things are known about early burial practices.

The contents of some Mogollon burials suggest that the Mogollon believed in life after death. Pots have been placed next to the bodies in their pit graves, which may mean that the dead were to use this pottery in their next lives. The Hohokam built platform mounds for religious ceremonies and they cremated their dead, including many sacred offerings, and buried the ashes in cream-colored bowls decorated with rust designs.

The Anasazi Basketmakers had tame dogs and the remains of two kinds of dogs have been found in human burials. One was a small black and white terrier-type and the other, a collie-like dog. Perhaps these animals were included in the graves so that the dead would have company on the journey to the next world.

For the Hopi, death is another step in life—another leaving of one world to come out into another.

The body of the deceased man is covered in deerskin; the woman, in her wedding clothes. A cloth mask symbolizing rain clouds covers the face. The body is put in a sitting position with the head between the knees. It is then carried out across the mesa to a grave that has been cut into the earth. No word is said as the body is placed in the hole, or as the bowl of food is put on a rock nearby. For four days, the women of the family mourn and daily bring food and *pajos* (pah´-hoes), prayer sticks, to the grave. Then village life returns to its usual patterns and the soul of the dead goes into the World Below to live with the Kachinas.

Notes for "Religion and Beliefs":

1. An elderly Santo Domingan woman said wistfully to me, "The best way for a Santo Domingan to die is dancin' the Easter dances. That way, you're already close to Heaven so you don't have far to go."

2. Another Pueblo Indian was perplexed that "you Whites don't always come to the dances when we invite you. (Dances are often on weekdays during work hours.) You just pass up all that (free) energy that we're offerin' you. I don't understan' you. . . . "

3. In Zuni, the children are taught that long ago all living things belonged to one family and this family was protected on all sides by six animals. In the north, the moun-

tain lion stood guard; in the east, the wolf; in the south, the badger; and in the west, the bear. Above, the eagle gave protection, and the mole kept watch below. These creatures were called the *Prey Gods* and little carved stone figures were made of them. These became the first handmade fetishes.

4. The Navajo reviewer of these materials wrote regarding this photo: "It is okay to use this photo in the book, but perhaps (you) should indicate that (this is the case as) the photo shows that *the medicine man* approved the presence of a foreigner *and* the photographing of the sing. (Besides,) the photo shows the boy sitting on paintings that have (already) been (partially) erased."

TRADE

In very early times, Southwestern people had little contact with strangers. Then gradually, about 2,000 years ago, traders from the south and occasional adventurers began to appear. This led to the exchange of commodities and the spread of new ideas.

The Mogollon were rather isolated from contact with their southern neighbors and so were not as influenced by outsiders as were the Hohokam who were active traders with people to the south.

The Hohokam made and used iron pyrite mosaic mirrors, stone palettes, truncated pyramids, large ball courts (which involved play with rubber balls), and they kept macaw parrots as housepets, all of which indicate a great deal of exchange between the Hohokam and the Indians from present-day Mexico.

You can imagine two prehistoric traders meeting on an isolated foot path. They don't speak a common language so they must communicate with hand gestures. One is an Anasazi from New Mexico and he carries two striking black and white pots each filled with chunks of turquoise. The other, a Hohokam from Arizona, holds a large ball of raw cotton, in which are nestled a variety of shell bracelets and necklaces. They barter their goods with one another and then each heads home, happy with the day's trade.

From about A.D. 100 on, goods were continually being brought to the pueblos by runners from the south. They carried seeds, plants, tobacco, new pottery designs—even fresh shrimp wrapped in moss and hand delivered from the Texas coast.

New Mexican pueblos, especially Zuni and Santo Domingo, played major roles in the Native trading network. This was because of their location midway between the Pacific and Atlantic coasts and halfway between the Meso-American and North American cultures. New Mexican turquoise was traded throughout the Southwest as well as Pueblo pottery—fragments of which have been found as far away as central Nebraska and Arkansas.

Shells from California and the Pacific coast were by far the most widely traded objects among prehistoric people. Both Olivetta and Conus shell beads made by the earliest Anasazi lay in caves of southern Colorado for nearly a thousand years. Cardium shells, probably used as containers, have been found in caves of southern Arizona.

In addition to objects, less tangible things were also exchanged. Successful working techniques spread from one group to another, as did rituals, songs, and even gods.

Occasionally, local tribal disputes interrupted the flow of trade, but then, in time, it would be reestablished. The trade system continued to function in this efficient manner until the time when the Spanish arrived.

"The old trade routes were as active as any of today's highways."

—Tesuque Pueblo man quoted in *Turtle Island Alphabet*

It is ironic to note that these ancient trade routes came to be used, thousands of years later, as the basis of many modern highways, which are in use today throughout the southwestern United States.

SOCIAL GROUPS AND GOVERNMENT

Early Native Americans of the Southwest lived together in small family groups. As the groups grew larger and, in the case of the Pueblo Indians, joined together in villages, more complicated rules for organizing community work and behavior were developed. The Spanish and the Americans brought with them other ideas of law and government, some of which were adopted into Native American life in this region.

SOCIAL GROUPS

The clan was the most important social group among the western Pueblos. Ownership of land and goods passed down from mother to daughter. (This is called a "matrilineal society.")[1] Three or four generations of women, their husbands, and their children might live in one household, in which the oldest woman was the most honored member.

Persons also had special relations with their father's clan, giving them more connections and opportunities than they received just through their mother's line. An important clan rule, which is still observed today, is that you must marry outside your own clan.

In Zuni, each clan had its special job to do for the whole village. Everybody in the pueblo had to work together to fill the community grainery in which food for all was stored for the winter.

There might be many clans living in one village; in some of the Rio Grande pueblos, the villages were also divided into two large social groups called *moieties* (a word anthropologists use to describe the two divisions within "a tribe"). Each moiety had responsibility for village activities for half the year. Santo Domingo (see Photo 37), for example, was divided into the winter people (turquoise, blue) and summer people (squash, yellow-orange).[2]

Photo 37. Adi Bandelier by Kiva at Santo Domingo; October 1, 1880. *Photo by G.C. Bennett, Bandelier College. Courtesy Museum of New Mexico (no. 4253).*

A Navajo is a life-long member of his or her mother's clan. But unlike the Pueblo people, Navajos did not live in villages. When a son married he usually chose to live near his mother and he would then build his hogan close by hers, where she, and her husband, children and sons-in-law lived.

The Apache bands that came into the Southwest spread across the land. No one group saw itself as a single united tribe. For example, the Chiricahua Apaches had three tribal groups; the Mescalero Apaches had five. Each tribal group divided itself into local groups of 10 or 20 large generational families. The Western Apaches had clans based on the mother's line of descent.

SOCIAL RITES

The people in these social groups took part in many ceremonies: some of these rites marked special times in their lives such as birth, coming of age, marriage, and death. The Apaches, for example, have a special four-day ritual that celebrates a young girl's coming of age. At the end of this ceremony, she is considered an adult in the community.

Girl Changing Into Woman

When a young Apache girl reaches child-bearing age she is honored with a special four-day ceremony that is held around July fourth. This is one of the most important times of her life.

It is believed that White Painted Woman created the first Changing Woman ritual "long ago when the flood had just left the land."

The young girl being honored wears a bright yellow doeskin skirt, blouse, and moccasins—symbols of pollen and fertility.

A wise older woman acts as the young girl's advisor. She tells her, "Be happy today so your people will be happy. Don't think bad thoughts or you'll have evil to the end of your days." Meanwhile, the White Painted Woman's holy shelter, a *wickiup*, is being built. Once it is completed, the girl, marked with pollen, enters her holy home. She is now, herself, White Painted Woman. Once inside, she lies down on a deerskin and is massaged by her advisor so that she may always be "flexible and happy."

During the next three days, the young girl will dance and will run in each of the four directions; she will stare at the sun and be blessed by the medicine man.

Each evening, the Mountain Spirit Dancers called *Gan* appear. (See Photo 38.) Around an enormous bonfire, these mysterious Gan perform. It is their role on each of the four nights to drive away any evil spirits that are present and to bless the crowd. The Gan impersonate spirits who have come down from certain nearby mountains and caves. Each dancer wears a black hood that completely covers his head and face. Tall headpieces, called *crowns*, top these masks. The participants hold sticks covered with symbols that they wave as they dance in the flickering firelight. The White Corn Maidens join the spirit dancers.

Photo 38. Mescalero Apache dancers, "Mountain Spirit or Devil Dance." *Courtesy Museum of New Mexico (neg. no 80063).*

On the fourth morning as the sun rises, the young woman faces east. With an eagle feather, the medicine man paints her face with white clay. Now she is certainly White Painted Woman.

Again she is brushed with pollen and again she runs in the four directions. Then her wickiup is pulled down and pushed to the east. Gifts are tossed to the crowd, candy to the young children, and her parents traditionally may now accept a marriage proposal on her behalf.

GOVERNMENT

The Spanish explorers were impressed by pueblo government, as they saw it. There were no chiefs, but each village had a kind of sheriff, which the Spanish called a *cacique* (cah-see´-kay) and several deputies who helped keep order in the village. They were guided by the advice of their oldest men, some of whom acted as priests, and were called *papas*.

Every morning at sunrise the priests at Zuni climbed the high terrace of the pueblo to preach to the people below, who listened in silence. The papas gave the people counsel on how to live and the Spanish believed this was the reason there was "no drunkenness . . . or human sacrifice . . . nor (did) they eat human flesh or steal."

The Spanish ordered the Indians to choose official representatives in each pueblo. These included a governor, lieutenant governor, *aguacil* (ah-gwah-seel´), "peace officer" and *mayor-domo* (my-yor-doh´-moh), "superintendent," each of which had special duties. The church officers were to be a *sacristan* (clerk) and a *fiscale* (fis-cah´-lay), "village spokesman" to the Spanish. These were the only people who could have official dealings with the Europeans. The Spanish were trying to make the pueblos become more European and "more civilized."

However, the Pueblo Indians used these new rules to hide the fact that they were actually continuing to govern themselves in the old ways! The Native priests chose as officers only those people who would see to it that the old ceremonial life continued strong and in secret. (See Photo 39.)

Photo 39. Restored Kiva at Spruce Tree House in Mesa Verde, Colorado; 1908. *Photo by Jesse L. Nusbaum. Courtesy Museum of New Mexico (neg. no. 60608).*

When the Americans came into power in the Southwest, they tried to force the Pueblo people (through religious and educational change) to become "good American citizens." The U.S. Government tried to get the pueblos to set up new systems of government that would separate religion and politics. It encouraged each pueblo to write a constitution. But the Pueblo people liked their old system of government in which religious power and political strength worked together as one. They didn't want to change their ways of ordering their lives in their villages. For over a century, this struggle continued.

Navajos and Apaches, not living in villages, had little need for governing bodies and officials. Problems that arose were taken care of locally, through discussion and with the help of an elder.

By the 1920s the Navajos were spread out over a very large reservation that the Bureau of Indian Affairs (BIA) divided into six areas. When a problem came up, the agent for the BIA would call a meeting with important Navajos from his division and they would work together to find a solution. Some problems, however, affected the whole Navajo nation. In 1922 it was decided to set up a tribal council that could represent all Navajos.

The Navajo Tribal Council was quite good at solving problems for the tribe, but it couldn't handle local situations that came up in all the far parts of the reservation. Another kind of governing organization was needed.

In 1927, local communities began to organize themselves into chapters. The people in each chapter elected officers who held meetings to solve local problems. This worked well. The Navajos had always solved disagreements by discussing them with local leaders, so the chapter system was just a new name for an age-old tradition.

As the Navajo population has grown, so has the size and responsibilities of the Navajo Tribal Council. In recent years the Navajo government has suffered from some problems of leadership at the higher levels.

Notes for "Social Groups and Government":

1. Some eastern pueblos had *patrilineal* groups where people traced blood relationships through their fathers. In these pueblos, the men controlled the property.

2. Anthropologists use this word *moiety* when they talk about each of the two main parts of a pueblo or tribe: one part will often be the dark (winter or turquoise); the other, the light part (summer or squash). Moieties are today part of the social groups in many of the Rio Grande pueblos.

   Taos Pueblo sits at the foot of the Sangre de Cristo Mountains of New Mexico. Taos people believe that they live at the top of the world because their sacred Blue Lake is located high on the edge of the mountains and according to their sacred teachings, it was through this lake that the very first people of Taos emerged.

   Taos can be seen as a clear illustration of the structure of a Pueblo society: Taos is divided by a running mountain stream into "North Pueblo" and "South Pueblo." The council of religious elders who administer the Taos tribe is taken in equal numbers from both halves and it governs impartially.

THE EUROPEANS COME

In the 16th century there were some 50,000 Pueblo people and 100 pueblo settlements in the Southwest.

At this time, Spanish expeditions came from Mexico in search of riches and gold (Coronado, de Niza, Esteban: 1540). They crossed Arizona and much of New Mexico. The Spanish did not find gold but they did make settlements (Juan Oñate: San Gabriel, 1598; later it became known as San Juan Pueblo). Life in the Southwest was hard and there was violence between the Spanish and the Acoma Indians.[1]

Then in the 17th century, the Spanish decided to begin converting the Native people to the Catholic faith—by force if necessary. Franciscan priests set up missions at the pueblos. In time, they controlled the lives of the Pueblo Indians who had to work for the livelihood of their own families *and* for the Spanish. Intertribal trading was badly disrupted and this weakened the Pueblo villages. The Spanish settlers had brought new diseases to the Southwest: measles, whooping cough, and smallpox. The Native people had no resistance to these. In 1640, almost 3,000 Pueblo people died of smallpox.

After years of mistreatment and slavery, the Pueblo people united in 1680 in a revolt that succeeded in defeating the conquerors and forced them out of the area. Nowhere else in the Americas did the Native people succeed in driving out the European invaders!

A dozen years passed. The Spanish began to return to the Southwest for both political and religious reasons. In 1689, the Spanish started to regain control over the Rio Grande Pueblo Indians. The Pimas rose up against the Spanish (1695) but were not successful in their efforts.

In the 1700s, the Spanish and Native Americans lived side by side and life was difficult for both cultures. But for the Pueblo people, it was especially hard. Raiding Apaches, Navajos, Utes, and Comanches upset their lives.[2] The Catholic priests outlawed their Pueblo religion so the people had to practice it in secret. Disease, drought, and starvation hounded them. From the original population of 50,000, the Pueblo people had dwindled to 14,000; 22 of the original 100 pueblo villages remained.[3]

In 1821, Mexico freed itself from Spanish rule. At that time, Mexican lands included present-day Texas, California, and the southwestern states.

In 1845 American settlers in Texas declared the independence of Texas from Mexico and the U.S. Army came "to protect Texas from Mexico." This eventually led to a U.S. declaration of war on Mexico in 1846.

Two years later, the U.S. and Mexico signed a peace treaty, The Treaty of Guadalupe Hidalgo, which gave Texas, much of California, and the present-day American Southwest to the United States.[4] Spanish-speaking people who stayed in these new U.S. territories became U.S. citizens, but citizenship for Native Americans was undecided at this time.

By 1850, the Pueblo population was at its lowest: only 7,000 Native people remained.

After the Civil War, Native Americans were still used as forced labor in mines and in logging areas of the Southwest.

Following the war, hundreds of newcomers moved in and it became almost impossible for roving Navajos and Apaches to survive. Then in 1862 the U.S. Army commander for the New Mexico Territory ordered the round-up of all raiding bands. They were given a choice: to live on a reservation—or be killed.

By 1864, about 8,000 Navajos had surrendered. They were marched 350 miles to Bosque Redondo, a reservation near the Pecos River. Four years later, after hundreds had died, the Navajos signed a peace treaty in return for the right to go back to their homelands.

Many Apaches had been taken to a reservation in Arizona. From time to time, some of them would escape and go on raids of wagon trains, towns, and farms. Bitter fighting between the Army and the Apaches continued until 1886 when Geronimo, the last warring Apache leader, was captured. A peace treaty was eventually signed.

Geronimo

The deadly struggle between the Native Americans and the European invaders had lasted for 300 years. For the most part, the Europeans failed to respect the unique culture of the Native people. They also did not accept the fact that the Native religion could be as central to these people's lives—and as heartfelt—as the Christian faith was to theirs. Treaties were signed and broken.[5] Many brave people died on both sides.

As devastating as the European invasion was, it did bring some positive changes and additions to the lives of the original inhabitants of these lands.

From the Spanish, the Native people got many important new sources of nutrition: melons; wheat; apple, peach, and pear trees; spices; certain peppers; and sugar. The domesticated animals (the horse, goat, donkey, cow, and sheep—whose wool was eventually used to make Navajo blankets) all came from Europe. Important inventions and discoveries such as the wheel, the working of iron and silver, guns, saddles, and cowboy-style clothing were all gifts from the Old World to the people of the New.

"There's not just one way of looking at history, but many ways. There's always two sides to a story."

—Dr. Greg Cajete, Santa Clara Pueblo, from the video *Surviving Columbus*

Notes for "The Europeans Come":

1. In 1599 in retaliation for the death of his nephew by some Ácomas, Commander Oñate had 70 armed Spaniards attack the pueblo. Between 600 and 800 Ácomas were killed. Surviving men and women were sentenced to 20 years of work for the Spanish. Young Ácoma men had one foot cut off. Sixty young women were sent to a convent and the children were put under the care of the Catholic priests.

2. These wandering bands had always lived by taking the goods of others. Their young warriors were taught that raiding was the courageous, intelligent—and admirable—way to live and prosper.

3. These figures are cited in the film *Surviving Columbus, The Story of The Pueblo People*, a two-hour PBS Home Video (No. 1016) available from KNME-TV Store, 1200 University Blvd., NE, Albuquerque, New Mexico 87102-1798. (Ask for current price before ordering.) This fine film would best be shown in half-hour segments to fourth graders (through junior high).

4. The Gadsden Purchase (1853) added more Mexican lands to the United States, including parts of Arizona, California, and New Mexico.

5. The Hopis remain the single Native American group to have never signed any treaty whatsoever with the United States Government.

And where are they today, the contemporary Native Americans of the Southwest? How do these descendants of the Mogollon and the Anasazi feed, clothe, and house themselves in the 20th Century? What aspects of their ancestors' lives still influence these people today?

THE DESERT INDIANS TODAY

In a time when nationally over half of the total Indian and Alaska Native populations live away from reservations,[1] the great majority of Southwest Native Americans remain close to their families and their ancestral birthplaces.[2]

Today, many Native Americans in the Southwest continue to farm and raise cattle, sheep and horses as their ancestors did. Others have taken jobs off the reservation in nearby big cities. Still others earn their living by producing silver and turquoise jewelry, pottery, rugs, or other fine arts or crafts.

FOOD

While the Pueblo and Navajo people enjoy hamburgers, French fries, and ice cream, they continue to eat corn, beans, and chile—some of which is home grown. But on the whole, they buy their food at the grocery stores. Although corn is seldom ground by hand today, many families do prepare Indian bread, piki bread, or Navajo fried bread. Some families are able to raise their own meat: beef, pork or mutton; others trade with neighbors for fresh meat. Although elderly people on the pueblos are eligible for such senior citizen benefits as free lunches via Meals on Wheels, the 1993 report on hunger in New Mexico stated that one in three elder Native Americans reported not having enough food to eat every month.

CLOTHING

Native American men in the Southwest often wear jeans and cotton shirts, cowboy boots, and cowboy hats as well as turquoise and silver jewelry. Of course, individual tastes vary. Many men wear Pueblo-style deerskin moccasins that fasten above the ankle with a leather thong or with silver buttons. Some men wear running shoes. Older men in winter may wrap a Pendleton[3] blanket around their shoulders, but down jackets are also popular!

The usual dress of a mature Navajo woman is a long-sleeved velvet shirt with silver buttons, or dime buttons, down the front. Her long velvet skirt with traditional vertical wrinkles falls about six inches from the ground. Turquoise and silver jewelry and Pueblo moccasins (or tennis shoes) complete her dress.

Older Pueblo women wear handmade, bright cotton print dresses of a traditional style, sometimes with one bare shoulder as in early times. A cotton or fringed lightweight wool shawl—or a sweater—may be worn over the dress. (See Photo 40.) Turquoise rings, necklaces, earrings, and Pueblo-style moccasins complete their outfits. In the cold months, bright-striped Pendleton blankets cover the heads and shoulders and are pulled about the body to keep out the chill.

Photo 40. Unidentified Navajo couple. *Courtesy Museum of New Mexico (neg. no. 3192).*

Young Native Americans wear the teenage fashions of the season and television often influences the current tastes—in music as well as in clothing!

SHELTER

While the Pueblo villages today look much as they did in the 19th Century, the traditional adobe houses have changed in some ways: glass windows have replaced sheets of mica; wooden doors have been added; linoleum covers dirt floors; and commercially made furniture is used in the rooms. Televisions, microwaves, and VCRs are becoming increasingly popular. Large glass cases often display family collections of jewelry, pottery, and blankets. Navajo rugs and wedding baskets are also displayed.

The Navajo are today the largest Native American group in the U.S. There are about 150,000 Navajos living on the largest U.S. Indian reservation, some 16 million acres of land. Many Navajos continue to live in traditional hogans, much like those of their early ancestors—except today the smoke hole has been replaced by a stove pipe chimney and the open fire by a wood stove. Even if a Navajo family has a modern tract house, they often also have a hogan nearby.

TOOLS

Today, farming on a pueblo often involves tractors, fertilizers, and soil-testing techniques. The pickup truck has usually replaced the daily use of a saddle horse.

Occasionally, a hand or pump drill will be used by a Native jeweler, but an electric drill from Sears is by far more common "because it drills a hole in a bead in a second."

Rifles have taken the place of bows and arrows, of course, and a chainsaw is often used in place of an axe.

LANGUAGE

It is believed that about one-third of all Native Americans in the United States still speak their Native languages.[4] Among these, the Navajos, Pima-Papagos, and Apaches show some of the highest percentages.

CRAFTS

Native American jewelers of today continue working in the spirit of their ancestors. The Santo Domingan turquoise overlay reminds us of Hohokam pendants, and their *heishe* (he´-she) bead necklaces are very similar to Anasazi shell and turquoise beads. Contemporary Zuni inlay jewelry uses tiny rectangles of turquoise shell, jet, and coral (which replaces the red argillite used by the Hohokam in *their* mosaic pieces). The Navajos continue to make striking silver and turquoise jewelry. (See Photo 41.)

Photo 41. Navajo Silversmith at Indian Inter-Tribal Ceremonial. Gallup New Mexico circa 1930. *Photo by W.T. Mullarky Courtesy Museum of New Mexico (neg. no. 27349).*

Today, the Papago make more baskets than any other tribe in the United States.

Both the Hopis and the Navajos make kachinas for commercial purposes. The Hopi kachinas are more detailed in carving, especially in the articulation of the hands.

Each pottery-making pueblo today produces pieces that are distinctive in glaze design from those of the other pueblos.[5] (See page 83.)

Navajos first made permanent sand paintings on particle board with a varnish covering as historical records because anthropologists said that the Navajo religion would otherwise be lost. They continue making these permanent sand paintings because they have become a tourist item and now some Navajos depend on this craft to make a living.

Sand paintings call forth the power of the Holy Ones only if they are exact reproductions of the holy designs. Commercial sand paintings sold as decorative objects will always have the colors or number of objects changed from those found in the original healing designs.

In our daily lives, most of the objects we use are mass-produced of inexpensive materials; when they break, become outdated or worn, we can easily replace them. The crafts made by Native Americans are examples of another way of thinking about time, craft, and art.

RELIGION

The Pueblo, Apache, and Navajo people continue to practice their Native traditions, ceremonial dances, and rituals that have been passed on from one generation to the next.

Today in the Southwest, many Native Americans practice both Christianity (usually Catholicism) as well as their Native American religion.[6] Both systems of belief teach their followers to love one another and both involve praying for people all over the world.

TRADE

Southwestern Native people continue, on the whole, to be open to the idea of trading (something they have made for materials or commodities they need or want). Money (and to a lesser extent, credit cards) are also commonly used.

Because the Navajo hogans are so remotely located, trading posts continue to be an important part of Navajo life. The posts offer groceries, utensils, yardage, blankets, tools, candy, and the most recent local news!

GOVERNMENT

Pueblo civil government is based on the early Spanish system. Each pueblo has a governor who is either elected or appointed for a one- or two-year period. There are one or two lieutenant governors and a sheriff. There is a treasurer whose duties involve both state and church. There is a war captain who is also a representative of the church. Finally, there is a council made up of former pueblo governors.

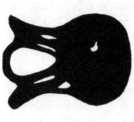

Navajo and Apache: Cooking Pot
Golden brown with
flecks of mica; may be
covered with pine pitch.

Santa Clara
Shiny black Wedding Vase

San Ildefonso
Black on red; also famous for
shiny black w/ indented design.

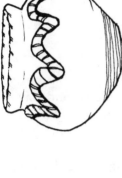

Zuni
White with rust & black

Taos and Picuris
Taos Bean Pot
Apricot-colored clay w/
flecks of mica in it.

Ácoma
Black & white olla

Laguna
Olla (water jar)
Black, white, rust

Tesuque
Heavy small pitcher

Santo Domingo
Heavy dough bowl
Black on white w/rust bottom.

Since the Europeans and Anglos came to the Southwest, the Native people have always found ways to poke fun at the settlers.

Today, Rio Grande potters make ceramic figures of the tourist wearing Bermuda shorts and sunglasses. The Hopis carve caricature kachinas; the Navajos weave, and make sand painting parodies of "the white men." Each year, Western Apaches give dramatic presentations in which they mock physicians, teachers, and VISTA workers. The Pueblo *koshares* (koh-shar´-ayz), or religious clowns, caricature young anthropology students as well as the U.S. President and Ronald McDonald!

In the 1920s a federal effort was made to completely integrate Pueblo and Navajo children into the dominant Anglo society. Native American children were forced to attend government-sponsored boarding schools and the young students were not allowed to speak any language other than English.

Despite such efforts, today Native American languages, the religious and cultural traditions, do prevail. As one elderly Santo Domingan man explained to me 20 years ago, *"We were here before you (Anglos and Hispanics) came . . . and we'll be here when you go."*

Notes for "The Southwestern Tribes Today":

1. *American Indians Today: Answers to Your Questions*, 1991, third edition, United States Department of the Interior, Bureau of Indian Affairs, Washington, D.C. 20240-0001, page 21.

2. *The Universal Almanac*, ed. by John W. Wright, published by Andrews & McMeel, 1993.

3. Pendleton Mills in Oregon has long produced bright-striped woolen blankets much favored by the Pueblo people.

4. Cited in *The Atlas of the North American Indian*, page 67, by Carl Waldman, published by Facts on File, New York, 1985.

5. For example, San Ildefonso Pueblo potters make black pots, often with a feather motif, and Santa Clara Pueblo makes black pieces with deeply incised designs. Cochiti Pueblo is famous for its storyteller figures as well as its whimsical animals. Ácoma potters continue to make ollas (large water pots) with traditional abstract designs. Zia ollas often feature birds. Hopi bowls are among the most valuable; they are cream or light tan in color, sometimes with a flush of peach on the sides. The designs and textured areas are dark brown or rust. In character, they are much like the bowls of the early Anasazi.

6. The Pueblo reviewer of these materials noted on the manuscript: "Our own religion is foremost in all practices. It always comes first. That's what my father told (taught) me."

HISTORIC NATIVE AMERICANS OF THE SOUTHWEST

Here are short biographies of two famous Southwestern native people: Nampeyo, the potter, and Geronimo, the warrior.

Following these are a list of additional Native American figures of the Southwest whose lives are intriguing and inspiring.

NAMPEYO: HOW ONE WOMAN BROUGHT BACK AN ANCIENT ART TO HER PEOPLE

One hundred years ago an archaeologist, J. Walter Fewkes, was digging up the ruins of a 14th-Century Hopi pueblo in northeastern Arizona. This pueblo had been destroyed, according to Hopi legend during a war over land and water, with the nearby pueblo of Walpi. At the time of this fight—to use Fewkes' own words, "The Hopi were making the best painted (pottery) ware of prehistoric North America." The shapes of this pottery were simple, yet elegant. The designs painted in red, orange, brown, and black were abstract and strong, and often covered the inside as well as the outside of the ceramic piece. (See Photo 42.)

On the Fewkes' digging crew was a Tewa Indian who was married to a part-Hopi woman named Nampeyo (Nom-pay´-yo). She had been taught by her grandmother to make very simple pottery. One night her husband brought home from the dig some broken pieces of pottery. He showed the ancient shards to Nampeyo—and her life was changed forever.

Photo 42. Nampeyo potter of Hano Pueblo; Hopi, Arizona; circa 1911. *Photo by H.F. Robinson. Courtesy Museum of New Mexico (neg. no. 21536).*

85

When she examined the clay pieces, Nampeyo was so struck by the fragmented designs that she promised herself that she would help bring back the art of Hopi pottery-making. So she studied the ancient clay pieces and began going to the dig to find shards herself. From these fragments, she reconstructed complete designs to fill the strong pottery shapes she now formed. With time, Nampeyo would say, "I used to go to the ancient village . . . to copy the designs, but now I just close my eyes and see the designs and I paint them."

In 1898, Nampeyo and her husband were invited to go to the Chicago Exposition to demonstrate her pottery-making. For the next 15 years, she continued to appear across America showing her art.

Then in 1920, Nampeyo's eyesight became so poor that she had to give up painting her pieces. But she had taught her daughters to make and paint pottery and so now she could form vessels and her daughters would then decorate them. They, in turn, began to teach her granddaughters to work in clay.

Today, Nampeyo's granddaughter, Leah, is passing on Nampeyo's gifts to a fourth generation of fine Hopi potters.

And so because one woman had an idea—a dream—and then worked to make it happen, generations after her continue to benefit from Nampeyo's efforts and artistry.

GERONIMO, "THE MOST CUNNING OF INDIAN FIGHTERS"

Born around 1829, Geronimo said in later life that as a boy he constantly "practiced stealing and the feats of war." (See Photo 43.)

Photo 43. Geronimo, Chiricahua Apache; 1905. *Photo by DeLancey Gill. Courtesy Museum of New Mexico (neg. no. 86991).*

Geronimo was not a Chiricahua, himself, but he married a Chiricahua Apache woman. Then one day on returning from a peaceful trading trip, Geronimo found that a band of Mexican raiders had come to his village and killed his wife, his mother, and his babies. Fueled by a deep desire for revenge, Geronimo rose to be a Chiricahua leader by exhibiting courage, skill, and determination in his struggles against the Mexicans.

In 1876 the U.S. Government removed the Chiricahuas from their mountain homeland in southeastern Arizona to the dry bottomlands of San Carlos Reservation.

In the fall of 1881 Geronimo and his band fled the reservation and hid in the Sierra Madre Mountains of Mexico. From there, they would make strikes on Mexican towns and up into southern Arizona, stealing, burning, and killing. The U.S. Army sent General Crook to Arizona. An experienced Indian fighter, Crook believed that only Apaches could catch Apaches, so he hired Chiricahua scouts and went into Mexico after Geronimo. It took two years to do it, but in 1884, Geronimo was forced back to the San Carlos Reservation.

The next year, Geronimo fled with about forty warriors and families. So General Crook returned to Mexico and, in 1886, Geronimo was forced to surrender, but he ran back to the Sierra Madre Mountains before the Army had even gotten him across the Mexican border.

General Crook was then replaced by General Miles. It took 18 months of pursuit by 500 Indian scouts and 5,000 Army troops to capture Geronimo, 8 boys, 101 women, and 35 Apache warriors. This time, the U.S. Army took no chances. They loaded their captives into wagons, put them on a train, and deported them from their Arizona homelands. Almost all of the Chiricahuas—those who had remained on the reservation, as well as Geronimo's band and, most cruelly, Crook's former Indian scouts—all were imprisoned; first in Florida, then in Alabama, and finally in Oklahoma.

Geronimo was put under military arrest at Fort Sill, Oklahoma. He was permitted to raise stock and to farm—unlikely occupations for a fierce fighter.

Geronimo later allowed himself to be exhibited at expositions in Omaha and St. Louis. He began wearing a top hat and rode with President Teddy Roosevelt in his inaugural parade in 1905.

Geronimo became a Christian and in 1906 he dictated his personal history to S. M. Barrett, *Geronimo's Story of His Life*. The next year he contracted pneumonia. Geronimo died in Fort Sill, in 1907, without ever seeing his Arizona homelands again.

OTHER IMPORTANT NATIVE AMERICANS OF THE SOUTHWEST

Louise Aberta Chewiwi, Laguna Pueblo writer, teacher

Conroy Chino, first U.S. Native American anchorman

Cochise, Chiricahua Apache chief

Helen Cordero, Cochiti potter

Frank C. Dukepos, Hopi scientist

Helen Hardin, Santa Clara Pueblo artist

Cochise

Ned Hatathli, Navajo Community College, founder and president

Fred Kabotie, Hopi artist (one of his paintings is reproduced in Photo 34)

Maria Martinez, Santa Clara potter

Pablita Velarde, Santa Clara Pueblo artist

Annie Wauheka, Navajo Tribal leader

Photo 44. Hopi artist Fred Kabotie; Hopi, Arizona. *Courtesy Museum of New Mexico (neg. no. 70435).*

THE
DESERT INDIANS

Activities for the Classroom

CRAFTS AND CLAY FUN

These craft-making suggestions have been included because each provides a sense of what it was like to deal with situations met by early people; each craft is educational and fun to do, and is possible to complete in a relatively short amount of time.

This is a terrific recipe for clay as it produces a material that is easy to form, fast drying, clean, and—once dry—rock hard!

Sand Clay Recipe

This recipe may be divided to provide 20 very small lumps for 20+ students. (When doubled the recipe produces a mixture that is, near completion, rather difficult to stir so use a big, strong [wooden] spoon and a pan from Goodwill.) You will need:

2 cups sifted sand

1 cup corn starch

1 1/2 cups cold water

Cook over medium heat, stirring constantly for 5 to 10 minutes, until mixture is very thick and not moist or sticky.

Turn onto a plate and cover with a damp cloth. Cool. Knead for a bit.

Sand clay may be kept indefinitely if double-bagged in plastic and refrigerated.

A Three-Dimensional Map

Make *two* double batches of Sand Clay. Once cool, wrap clay tightly in a plastic bag and tie off; then put clay inside a second bag so that the clay will remain moist.

Divide the class into pairs so that two students work together on constructing each map. Each pair of students will then be given:

a large piece of foamcore or heavy cardboard (scraps of these are often free from framing shops)

a copy of the map from "How the First People Came Here" activity sheet

white glue

toothpicks

2 plastic picnic knives

2 pencils

2 small balls of Sand Clay

Have the students study the map and, using pencils on foamcore, make a large outline of the land masses shown on the map. (Next they may apply some white glue to the middle area of their drawing to help anchor the clay once it is applied.)

One ball of Sand Clay is smoothed out onto their land mass drawing. Stay within the boundaries and smear the clay so that it is thinner near the edges of the map outline and thicker in the interior of the map.

Now the two students use the second ball of clay to build up the high areas and mountains; they should refer to the map constantly to keep their 3-D map accurate. The plastic knives and toothpicks are used to create crevices, rivers, plains, and lakes. Encourage the teams of students to *cooperate* in constructing these maps; both students of each pair should be involved in the molding of the map contours.

Put the maps out of the way (near a heat source) and check periodically to note dryness. Once dry, these maps can be given light coats of watercolor; the ocean areas can be painted by using poster paint or watercolor. Use a toothpick to apply white glue under any area that may pull away from the cardboard. Finally, the mapmakers should create a neatly printed title on their map that includes the signatures of the two cartographers.

Fossils and Prehistoric Creatures

If possible, have actual fossils on display. Make a batch or two of Sand Clay, and wrap it tightly in a plastic bag and then in foil to keep it moist. Have each child collect small objects to use in their fossil making: small shells, feathers, leaves, and bones work very well. A student may work to construct a small prehistoric animal by gluing some bones, feathers, toothpicks or balsa wood strips together. Each child gets a lump of Sand Clay, then experiments while making impressions in the clay. Some children may want to build small prehistoric creatures from the clay. Remind them to adhere appendages by smearing clay on all the seams, not just butting a leg against the clay body. Toothpicks can be inserted inside clay to connect a leg to a body. Let the clay dry well overnight on a cookie sheet near a heat source before moving the student-made fossils.

Pottery

Sand Clay is excellent for using to form small pinch pots (a ball of clay is pinched in the middle to form the inside of pot and the walls of the pot are pinched upward). A catalog of different types of tiny pots used as toys by Hopi girls can also be created.

Hopi Toy Pottery

Once the pot is dry, poster-paint designs can be added. (Just be careful not to soak the pot with moisture or it may crack.)

Jewelry

You will need for each child: Sand Clay and a bamboo skewer (packs of these are sold at grocery stores for shish kebabs or barbecues). Have the students study the various prehistoric bead shapes you copy onto the chalkboard.

Stone Beads
(of early Pima)

Students roll the clay into small balls and shape these into beads. The skewer is used to pierce each ball (and then the skewer is twisted around and around to make a clean hole through the bead). Skewers are used to indent clay and create a pattern on each bead. Beads are allowed to dry completely before stringing them on cord or thin leather thongs.

Prehistoric-style pendants can also be made in this way and, once dry, combined with beads to make striking necklaces.

Etched Shell Beads
(Pima)

Fetishes: Animal Helpers

Have the students study various photos/pictures of fetishes (in books or) which you draw on the chalkboard. Have each child see which fetish animal they seem most drawn to, and then, using Sand Clay, replicate this figure. Once fetishes are completely dry, feathers and "arrowheads" may be bound to them.

Animal Helpers:

Bear   Frog   Birds   Fox   Turtle

Navajo Mud Toys

These can be replicated once children have studied the traditional shapes of these figures. Once the mud clay is dry, the Navajos wrap raw wood (brown, black, grey, or white) around the sheep figures to give them a naturalistic touch.

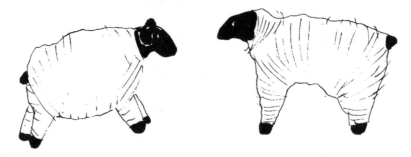

Navajo Mud Toys
Sun-dried mud bodies are wrapped snuggly with raw wool.

Sand Paintings

You will need fine white sand (from a builders' supply store) or cornmeal, 2 dozen baby food jars with lids, different colors of food coloring (or tempera mixed rather thin with water), rectangles or squares of corrugated cardboard (e.g., 6″ x 8″, etc.), white glue, and scratch paper and pencil for each child.

Fill each little jar 3/4 full of sand (or cornmeal). Drop food coloring or tempera of a different color into each (2) jars. Screw a lid onto each jar and shake up sand (cornmeal) well. (Add more coloring if needed.) Continue to shake jar through morning until sand (meal) is colored, and then let it dry.

Have the students look at some Native American symbols such as those below and ask them to each draw one of these symbols (to fill the area of the cardboard) on scratch paper first. You will need to check to see that each design is bold (no tiny details) and large enough to nearly fill the cardboard. If this is the case, the student uses a pencil to then draw this design onto the cardboard square.

Next an area of the design, which will be one color, is given an all-over coat of white glue; this coating should be wet but not running and should neatly touch all of its outlines. A handful of colored sand or cornmeal is sprinkled on the area and is allowed to stand for a few minutes. Then any excess sand (meal) is gently shaken off the cardboard and funneled back into the appropriate jar. Finally the jar's lid is screwed on again. This

process is repeated with each successive color until the entire surface of the cardboard is covered with colored substances.

Older students will be able to apply glue to the several areas that will be one color and cover all these areas with cornmeal or sand at one time.

Some areas of cardboard may be left bare as a contrast in texture and tonality. Allow these sand paintings to dry *completely* before displaying them. (A light coat of spray Verathane can be given to each *dry* painting as an added protective covering.)

Ask older students what, if anything, their sand paintings have in common with Navajo sand paintings. Be open to all their suggestions.

Be sure your students understand that their paintings are simple designs inspired by the Navajos' very complex and religious sand paintings—which are never permanent, but are made to be used and then erased that same day!

Sand Painting Variations

Instead of cardboard, use sheets of fine sandpaper as the backing to which the colored sands are glued. Contact the woodshop teacher at your local high school and ask if he or she can suggest an inexpensive source of fine sandpaper.

Natural Clay

In some areas of the country, you can dig the clay yourself straight out of the ground or riverbed. Otherwise, look in the Yellow Pages under Pottery Supplies or ask a potter where clay can be bought in quantity, usually fifty-pound bags. A variety of color is available (depending on where you live), ranging from oranges, reds, and greens into the browns.

Eventually you will find yourself wanting access to a kiln. Ask potters in the area if you might work out an arrangement for firing, or perhaps a parent may be able to help with advice as to glazing and firing.

Here is the way some present-day Zuni Pueblo potters fire their pottery—and with a little effort your *class* may, too!

How to Make an Open Pit for Firing Pots

an open area of ground

shovels

dried twigs and small logs

optional: cookie sheets

medium sized logs

matches

Dig a shallow pit in the ground and have the children gather dried twigs and small pieces of wood. Place completely dried pots* on the bottom of the pit. Separate them, one from another (with pieces of broken pottery). Cover the pots with lots of small twigs and then add medium-sized pieces of wood. Set the wood on fire. Add larger pieces of

---

*You can put the pots on cookie sheets in a low oven for an hour to be sure that they are absolutely dry and will not explode later in your pit firing.

wood as the fire burns down. You may place sheets of metal over the burning wood to help conserve the heat.

Prepare the children for the possibility that some pots may break during the firing: "But it doesn't matter at all; we will just make some new ones and do another firing."

After an hour, allow the fire to die out and remove the pots when they are cool. These vessels are more suited for ceremonial, rather than eating, purposes. They make good incense burners, dried-weed holders, or *objets d'art*.

Symbols

Because they believed all natural things—all trees, pottery, animals, baskets, plants, everything—had a living spirit, the Native Americans thought each of these spirits could be spoken to through the use of symbols. A picture of a rain cloud on a pottery bowl was a request for rain. The circle, itself, was a favored decoration as it symbolized the connection between all things in life!

To create a symbol in the way Native Americans did, choose a bird, fish, plant, reptile, or animal and carefully study the way its body is put together. Decide on one or two important parts you want to emphasize. Make a very simplified outline drawing of your creature; try not to include small details. Then exaggerate the one or two important parts: you can do this by drawing them larger or giving them more color than the rest of the creature.

Look at these Pueblo drawings to see how those early people created symbols:

Now choose one of these pottery shapes and make a large drawing of it and carefully decorate it using your symbols (and other lines).

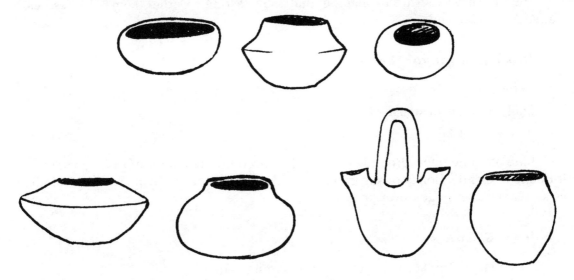

Earthen Clay Paint

different shades of dried clay (from chocolate brown to yellow ochre, rust and porcelain white)

water

hand-sized stones

big square of wood or heavy cardboard

a bowl

containers with lids to hold the various colors of clay paint

Grind the dried earthen clay with the stones, pressing clay against the wooden or cardboard square. Mix pulverized clay with water in a bowl until it is of a paint-like consistency. Store it in a container until the paint is used to decorate "ceremonial" pots (*not* to be used for cooking) or to create large prehistoric paintings on big pieces of cardboard.

Yucca Paintbrushes

If you live where yucca grow, you can make paintbrushes much like those used by the Mogollan! Tear a spear of yucca (or other nonpoisonous fibrous plant) lengthwise into narrow strips. Bind the lengths into a bundle with yarn, wrapping the stalks several times and tying them securely. With a sharp rock, scrape and fray the ends of the bunch, using water to soften the fibers. The result resembles the hairs of a brush.

Clean-up for all clay activities can be done with warm water, buckets and sponges. Get everybody to help!

FOOD PREPARATION

While we cannot duplicate the conditions under which Native Americans did their cooking (an open pit fire or outdoor oven) and food preparation (drying corn on the rooftops of their adobe pueblo buildings), we can encourage our students to experience and understand the processes involved in early Southwestern food preparation.

You can have the fun of making, and then tasting together, some of these early Native American foods.

Gruel/Atole (ah-toh´-lay)

water

finely ground cornmeal

honey (or sugar)

Blue or white finely ground cornmeal is stirred into boiling water and cooked until it thickens slightly. Honey or sugar may be added. This is drunk by many Pueblo Indians as a breakfast beverage—even today.

Dried Squash

2 to 3 large, firm squash (Butternut or summer squash)

string or cord

optional: chicken broth, salt, butter

Wash, dry, and peel 2 to 3 large squash. Slice squash horizontally in 1/4″ slices so that the middle hollow forms a hole within each slice. Remove the seeds.

String the squash slices on a piece of sturdy cord and tie this like a clothesline in a dry sunny place. Separate the squash slices so air can circulate between them.

Once dried, squash slices can be kept in a covered container and then added to soups, stews, or chicken broth as it simmers. Serve warm with salt and butter.

Beef Jerky* (a two-day process)

1 1/2 lbs. brisket of beef or a large flank stake

1/4 cup soy sauce

1/2 cup water

1 tsp. garlic, freshly squeezed

1/2 cup onions, finely minced

1 Tbsp. brown sugar

Partially freeze the meat to facilitate cutting. Remove all fat. Slice the meat across the grain into *thin* slices. Combine the above ingredients in a big bowl and place the meat strips in this liquid overnight, turning occasionally. The next day remove the meat from the liquid and shake off any excess moisture. Place these strips directly across the racks of your oven. Heat the oven to 150-200° for 3 to 7 hours until the beef slices are thoroughly dried or jerked.

---

*To jerk means to preserve by drying. We get our word jerky from the Spanish *charqui* (char´-ke) who encountered it in Peru where charqui means meat dried in strips.

Beef jerky may be stored in a covered container, but the children will probably want to begin chewing on it at once—just as Native Americans did long ago!

Dried Corn

6 cups chicos (*chee´kohs*)*

boiling water

2 Tbsp. butter

salt

optional: 2 Tbsp. sugar

Pour boiling water, to cover, over the chicos. Soak for an hour *or more*. Then place over moderate heat; simmer for one-half hour or until kernels are soft enough to chew. Add the butter and salt to taste. (Sometimes sugar is added to the simmering corn, if you want a more confectionery flavor.)

Chicos were eaten by the Pueblo people throughout the winter months.

SHELTERS

Creative Interpretations of Early Shelters

Provide the student with a variety of materials such as: large sheets of corrugated paper (sides of appliance packing boxes), odd sheets of plywood, hot glue guns, white glue, ice cream sticks, fine sand, a variety of small boxes, dried twigs, grass, paintbrushes, milk cartons of different sizes, tempera paints, scissors, (Homemade or Cooked) Play Dough, and construction paper.

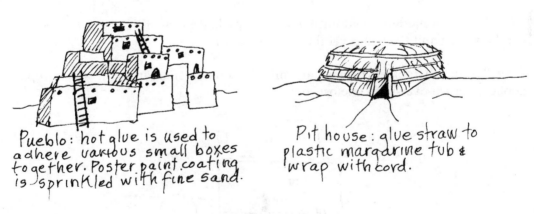

Pueblo: hot glue is used to adhere various small boxes together. Poster paint coating is sprinkled with fine sand.

Pit house: glue straw to plastic margarine tub & wrap with cord.

Old style Hogan

*Available in the Southwest or in specialty food shops, these dried sweet corn kernels are added to beans or homemade soup as it simmers.

In addition to completing the Shelter activity sheets, students can create their own personal interpretations of southwestern architecture and shelters. The students first explore the various materials that are laid out on a large table or area. Then they review the various shelter structures (pit house, hogan, wikiup, kiva, ramada, pueblo, cliff dwellings, ki). Encourage them to work in small groups to create early villages or structures near the fields. Let them originate various approaches.

Homemade Play Dough

4 cups flour

1 cup salt

8 Tbsp. salad oil

7 to 8 Tbsp. water

food coloring

Stir together and knead. Add food coloring. Keep securely wrapped in plastic when not in use.

Cooked Play Dough

2 cups flour

2 Tbsp. salad oil

1 cup salt

4 tsp. cream of tartar

2 cups water

food coloring

Cook over medium heat until a soft lumpy ball forms. Knead until smooth. (Dough can be frozen and thawed several times to keep.)

Play dough molded over small milk cartons or margarine tubs can replicate an adobe or brush-over-mud enclosure.

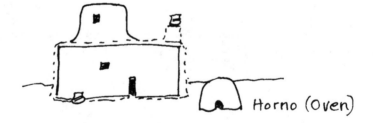
Horno (Oven)

Pueblo Levels

Various pueblo levels can be cut from cardboard and hot-glued together. These can be painted with (thickened) poster paint and sprinkled with sand, then repainted with poster paint to achieve adobe-like texture.

A Classroom Exhibit

Once a variety of miniature shelters has been created, ask for volunteers to form a committee that will be responsible for organizing the student-made shelters into a classroom exhibit. Explain that you will provide any art materials they request, free time in which to set up the exhibit, and extra credit points (if these are offered in your classes).

TOOL-MAKING IDEAS

Provide a supply of the following: little sticks, dead wooden matches, small scraps of wood, lots of sandpaper, scissors, white glue, markers, thin leather scraps, waxed carpet thread, cotton string, small pieces of netting, needles, thread, small round rocks, big buttons (for hand-drill balancers), and long reeds (for atl-atls).

Have the students study pictures of prehistoric tools (see "Tools" section earlier in this book). Provide the materials listed above and encourage the class to bring in specific sticks or pieces of wood, shells, leather, etc., that they think would work well as (part of) a tool.

Finally, when a wide selection of materials has been collected, ask each child to select a tool to faithfully and carefully reproduce. Give the class adequate time for this project so students will not feel rushed.

When (a selection of) the tools has been completed, ask students to come up with suggestions for exhibiting their work and sharing these handmade tools with other classes. Ask for a volunteer who (for extra credit) will lead the group discussion and oversee the selection of an ultimate solution for organizing, labelling, and exhibiting these prehistoric tool replications.

Digging Stick

Stone Knife with wooden handle.

Foot was placed here & stick was shoved into the ground. Point was charcoaled

Sand clay can be used by the children to form realistic-looking bird points, arrowheads, scrapers, drills, small axeheads, small manos and metates, or small Hohokam paint palettes. Encourage the students to include every detail of the original prehistoric tools.

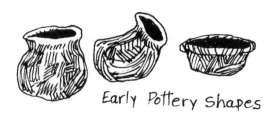

Early Pottery Shapes

Navajo Cooking Pot
is scraped with a
corn cob & lined
with piñon resin.

Projectile Points

   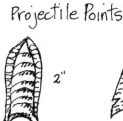   

Clovis 3″
9500 BC

Folsom 2″
9000 BC

HohoKam 2″- 4″
AD600-1400

Pueblo 1″
AD700-1050

WEAVING

a wide variety of wool yarn

scissors

6″ x 7″ mat board scraps or shallow Styrofoam meat trays (mat board scraps often come free from framing shops)

cotton string

optional: 4″ plastic blunt-ended needles (available at yarn and craft stores)

optional: plastic combs for tamping down woven threads on loom

optional: fake fur, long leaves, grasses, feathers

Cardboard looms can be prepared ahead of time. On the 6″ ends of the mat board, mark uniform intervals of 1/2″. These marks can be 1/4″ apart for older children. Make an equal number of marks at the opposing end. Use scissors to make a 1/2″ deep cut on each mark.

To string the loom, make a slipknot at one end of the cotton string and lace it over the first slit (at the backside) of the loom. Next bring the string down the front of the loom to the bottom and insert it through the first slit there, hooking it behind the support, and up through the second slit. Then bring the string back up the front of the loom to the top and through the second slit there. Again, behind the support and through the third slit.

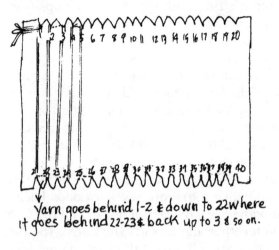

Yarn goes behind 1-2 & down to 22 where it goes behind 22-23 & back up to 3 & so on.

Continue this way until the loom is strung. (Be careful *not* to string the warp around the front and back of the mat board as this makes it difficult to remove the finished weaving from the loom.) When you have strung the entire loom, secure the end of the string with another slipknot and snip it from the ball of string. Older students will be able to string the warp on their own looms.

Very young children will use lengths of yarn slightly longer than the loom is wide, a bit less than a foot long. To cut the yarn, get a piece of cardboard half the length of the proposed yarn length. Wrap the yarn, straight from the ball, around and around the cardboard twenty or thirty times. Then, with sharp scissors, make one even cut through the bunch; you now have thirty pieces of your desired length.

Once the yarn and looms are ready, pass out the looms (and the threaded yarn needles for little kids). Older students will select their own choice of yarn. Demonstrate how to start at the bottom of the loom, at either the right or left side. The first and most important concept is *over/under* for one row (over the first warp string and under the next) switching to *under/over* for the next row, alternating with every row and pressing down the yarn in each row as it is woven. At first, young children may forget to alternate the over/under pattern with each new row. If this pattern is not followed, the weaving falls apart when removed from the loom.

Once a row is completed, it is easiest for the beginner to trim the strand if it is too long, leaving a little fringe of 1/2″ to 1″ on either side. Then slide the strand down to the very bottom of the loom. Each new row is pressed down in this way—and so the weaving grows.

Older students will use very long lengths of yarn and may choose to intersperse natural elements (long grasses, hemp twine, thin bark) into their weavings as they go along. Encourage them to select yarns that compliment the colors of these pieces of nature.

Tiny weavings may be made on 2″ x 4″ pieces of mat board. They take much less time to complete and so they are very appealing to six- and seven-year-olds!

Mounting the Finished Weaving

Each child will need two thin sticks a bit longer than the weaving, sandpaper to smooth these, and cotton string. Unhook the warp loops from the loom, first one end, then the other. It is usually necessary to condense the woven mass by pressing the outside rows more toward the center so as to gain a little extra margin in the loops.

Start the stick through the loops, twisting each loop once before passing the stick through it. When both top and bottom sticks are in place, smooth the weaving back out, spreading it up to the sticks for a secure hold. Tie a length of string to the ends of the top stick to form a loop to use for hanging the weaving on the wall.

Belt looms allow students to weave belts for themselves! Have each child measure his or her waist and then add 8″ or 9″ to this figure. Cut a 1″ x 1″ or 2″ x 2″ board to this length. Tack little finishing nails at either end, about 1/4″ apart. String the warp with cotton string. Use a blunt-ended darning needle and weave the basic *over/under*, *under/over* pattern, taking care to work the yarn ends back into the main part of the weaving to ensure smooth edges. Be careful not to pull the yarn too tight (this draws the warp strings too close together and distorts the line of the belt). A plastic comb can be used to keep the strings separated during the weaving process.

Loom Variations

The Navajo upright loom can be approximated on a small scale by the hanging dowel loom.

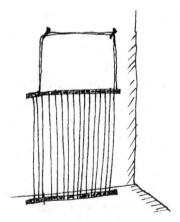

Other simple looms include the box lid loom and the plastic or paper plate loom!

Paper plate with slits around edge for stringing of warp threads. Weaver starts at center, moving outward toward edge of plate.

Box with sides indented for easier access of hands.

SAND TRAY STORIES

How to Make a Sand Tray

the lid of a sturdy cardboard file box (or cut off the bottom of a sturdy cardboard box leaving a 2 1/2″ lip all the way around the box bottom

an X-acto™ knife

duct tape

pile of newspapers

ruler

pencil

pane of single-strength glass about 11″ x 12″

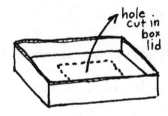

hole cut in box lid

Place the cardboard lid on top of the pile of newspapers so that it acts as a cushion when you cut through the lid. Use the ruler and pencil to measure off a 9″ x 9″ square on the inside of the lid. Use the X-acto™ knife to carefully cut along the pencil lines. Remove the inside square.

Next place the glass pane over the cut-out area in the lid. Use the duct tape to cover all the edges of the glass and secure it to the cardboard. Turn the lid over and tape the glass to the cut-out area using the duct tape.

GLASS Duct Tape

holds glass over hole & reinforces cardboard

You may also want to reinforce with tape all of the lid's lip inside and out as the Sand Tray gets a lot of use and the lip may eventually get split or crumpled.

To use your Sand Tray, you will need an overhead projector, fine (sifted) sand (from a sandbox or a bag of fine sand from a building supply store which is very inexpensive), various transparent colored plastic sheets used as notebook dividers or pieces of colored cellophane, a sturdy piece of cardboard 4″ x 11″ to rake across the sand and erase the last picture, a large cardboard comb 4″ x 11″ to draw through the sand to produce a wave pattern, and a tiny flashlight to help you read the script in the darkened room.

Place the box lid with the glass panel on top of the glass of the overhead projector. Pour in part of the sand—experiment to get the right amount of sand—enough to black out the light of the overhead projector, but not so much that the sand falls down and fills in the lines as you draw them with your finger or thumb.

Occasionally place a (doubled-over) piece of cellophane just above the lines in the sand to change the color of the projected image.

"Erase" the lines by smoothing the sand with your hand or the side of the cardboard, or by leveling the sand by gently shaking the tray.

REMEMBER: You need to draw the pictures upside down! Watch the pictures you make as they are projected on the wall (screen) to see how you can improve your technique with this sand tray.

Eventually you—or your students—may come up with variations for making lines and creating visual effects on the Sand Tray. (Try blowing through a straw into a line drawn in the sand for a starter. . . .)

A Sand Tray Story

(*Turn out the lights*).
(The underlined words will be shown as drawings on the sand tray.)

Kokopelli (Koh-koh-pe´-ee) the Hump-Backed Flute-Player and How He Led the Hopis to Their New Home

When the Hopi people <u>came up out</u> of <u>the sipapu</u> (see-pah-poo´) into the Fourth World, the Great Creator told them that they would have to go out into all of the <u>four directions</u> before they would come to that place that would be their actual new home.

There are many stories of their travels and many of these stories speak of an insect person who was their guide: <u>Kokopelli </u>was his name. He was a <u>grasshopper</u>. He was also a flute-player—and sometimes a trickster as this story will show you.

There are many petroglyphs of Kokopelli—carvings on the rocks in North and South America, Mexico, and Canada. The Hopi people say that this proves how far they traveled before they finally came home to their Hopi land.

Well, in the beginning Kokopelli took the Hopi up a steep <u>mountain</u>. And at the top of this mountain there was a huge <u>eagle</u>.

"I stand guard over this part of the world and I have been here since the first. If you want to go in this direction, you must pass my test."

Kokopelli stepped forward. "The Hopi people want to live in this land," he said. "I am ready. Test me."

The eagle drew out a <u>long arrow</u> and he <u>drove it through his body</u>. It came out through his back and yet there was no blood to be seen.

"All right," said Kokopelli, "that should be easy." So <u>he took the arrow and placed it under his wing covers so that it **LOOKED** like it had gone through him and come out the other side.</u>

"Yes, I see that you have great powers!" said the <u>Eagle</u>. "You all have my permission to go into your new homeland. Also, from today on, you may use my <u>feathers</u> to make your <u>prayer sticks</u>. My feathers will take your prayers quickly up to the Creator."

So it is that ever since that day, the Hopis have <u>placed eagle feathers on their pahos</u> (pah´-hohs), their prayer sticks.

Then it was that <u>Kopkopelli </u>led the Hopi people <u>into their new land</u>. As he walked along, he played his flute and so the land and the winds became warm. In the hump on his back Kokopelli carried seeds of all our native plants. So it is that the <u>corn</u> and <u>beans</u> and <u>squash</u> and all the <u>spring flowers</u> began first to grow in the Southwest.

The Hopi people traveled for many weeks with the Hump-backed Flute-Player. Together they walked across the beautiful Fourth World in those early days.

Read over the Kokopelli story and decide how you will illustrate it on the sand tray. Here are some suggestions:

You may add any other symbolic pictures you wish.

EARLY NATIVE AMERICAN GAMES

Here is a collection of games played by the early Southwestern peoples that you may enjoy playing with your students. As you play these games you are sharing in their lives—even across the centuries!

How Many Knots?

For this guessing game you will need a length of thin rope 18″ long for every two players.

Each two players sit facing one another with a distance of about 8 feet between them. One child holds the rope out in front and the other player, who is the guesser, says at some point: "Ready." At once the first child puts both hands and the rope behind his or her back and quickly ties any number of single knots in it, from none to four. When the knots are completed, the child brings the empty hand back in front and the other child guesses the number of knots on the rope. The guesser only gets one guess.

Immediately the rope is brought out in front to show the true number of knots. If the guesser was correct, she or he now gets to repeat the game as the knot-maker this time. If the guesser was incorrect, the knot-maker gets to try and fool the opponent a second time.

Basket Catch

You will need an 8″ to 12″ in diameter shallow basket (or if none is available, a wide-mouthed wooden salad bowl) and six heavy cardboard disks: 1 1/2″ in diameter with numbers or symbols indicating from 1 through 6 on one side and, on the reverse side, one of each of these: 2-4-6-0-0-0 on each of the six disks. The early pueblo people used rounded pot shards as their gaming pieces!

Potshard Gaming Pieces

The players, all but one who remains standing through the game, sit cross-legged in a circle on the floor. The basket of disks is given to one of the seated players who grasps it in both hands and quickly, from lap level, tosses the disks into the air and then attempts to catch as many as possible in the basket, without changing his or her sitting position! The score made on each throw (the total of all the numbers left showing at the end of the throw) is counted out loud by the standing player. The basket is then passed to the next seated player in the circle and play continues. The player at the end of all play who has the highest score is the winner. Sometimes a second round of play between two players must happen in order to break a tie in scores.

Basket Toss

This is a variation on "Basket Catch" and requires the same materials plus a second basket of the same size as the first.

The game is played in pairs and the two players sit facing one another about four feet apart. The first player holds a basket with the numbered disks and immediately after calling out, "Ready!" he or she sharply jerks the basket up and forward in the direction of the player opposite, tossing the disks into the air. This second player, without leaving the sitting position, catches as many disks as possible in the basket that she or he holds.

Different methods for doing this are possible: you can place the basket under the disks as they fall downward or you can point the bowl of the basket toward the flying disks and intercept them in the air. Disks that fall to the ground or out of the basket don't count. The score is based on the points shown on the uppermost faces of the disks as they land in the basket.

Play is then repeated in reverse with the catcher becoming the disk-tosser. These two players are considered to be partners and it is their joint score that will be in competition with the other partner-pairs playing the game.

Koshare, or Clown, Ball

The Zuni clowns or koshares (koh-shar´-ees) lend a lighthearted humorous side to the ceremonial dance offerings. Koshare Ball is a game they play with slapstick gestures and pratfalls to amuse the Pueblo observers and their visitors.

A long center line, running North to South, is drawn in the dirt of the playing area. This outline is carefully filled in with cornmeal. To either side of this line, and at a distance of 15 feet* to each side, another line is drawn, to finally form three parallel lines.

The players line up, three feet apart, half of them behind the Eastern line and half behind the Western line. One side is given a cloth-covered semi-hard ball that is 6″ in diameter. The player with the ball runs to the center line and throws the ball, trying to hit any player on the opposing team. If a player is hit, he or she goes over to the thrower's side. Immediately upon hitting the player, the ball is retrieved and returned to the successful thrower who continues to throw until he or she misses. The opposite team then gets the ball and is allowed to throw until it misses. (This is where the Koshares' antics take over: They appear to be silly and clumsy while they cleverly dodge and bluff to avoid leaving the line **AND** to avoid being hit by the ball!)

Play continues until one team is totally depleted and forced to join the opposing team. (Sometimes this is not possible in a school setting and a specific time limit must halt the play.)

EARLY SOUTHWESTERN TOYS

Bullroarer

This soundmaker was used as a toy and also as part of very sacred ceremonies. The sound this object produced called up images of thundering clouds, the voices of gods, as well as, the roar of a bull.

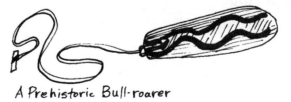

A Prehistoric Bull-roarer

---

*This distance would be marked off prior to the students gathering on the field for play.

For each noisemaker, you will need a long sturdy stick or dowel, a three-foot long piece of strong (leather thong) cord, a drill, sandpaper, and a rectangle of thin strong wood into which you have drilled four holes.

Sand the wooden rectangle well so that no rough or pointed corners or edges remain.

Tie one end of the cord to the wooden rectangle and the other end to the stick as shown. (Sticks were not always used in prehistoric times, but for safety measures are a good idea for student-made bullroarers.)

Hold one end of the dowel firmly in hand and, by making a swift circular motion, cause the wooden piece to soar—and roar!

Have the students experiment with varying sizes and numbers of holes in the wooden pieces. This, and different placements of holes, will produce a variety of sounds. Encourage the children to try and explain how and why these sound changes occur.

Cradle Kachinas[1]

paint mixing sticks

wooden tongue depressors

hot glue gun (or white glue)

markers

poster paint

yarn

fake fur scraps

little fluffy white feathers

scissors

Verathane spray

saw with which to cut each piece in half

Have the children study a variety of Cradle Kachina photos and pictures in books,[2] or you can make copies of these and the Cradle Kachinas on page 56, and hand them out among the class. Ask each child to choose one they will then make as a little flat Kachina doll.

Provide all the art materials listed above and let each student interpret his or her Kachina individually. Emphasize neatness and clarity of color when paint is applied to the wood. Use of the hot glue gun must be supervised and is appropriate for use only with mature students. Once the Cradle Kachina is finished, it is given a light coat of Verathane to protect the colors. The yarn around its neck (by which it is hung to the cradleboard), and any feathers it may have, are added at the very last.

The name of the Kachina and its maker's name are printed in thin black letters at the bottom of the back of the doll.

(A bulletin board display of all the children's kachinas would be outstanding. Simply suspend each doll by stapling the yarn loop around its neck to the bulletin board. The title of this display could be: *Cradle Kachinas, the first toys of Hopi Indian babies.* (Little dolls such as these are hung from a Hopi baby's cradleboard. Each doll has a lesson for a Hopi child.) Include a map next to the display and circle Hopi Mesas on it so students will see where these toys originate.

Huwawanani

This whirling toy was commonly played with by early Southwestern Hopi children. They made a Huwawanani by threading a loop of heavy cotton string through two holes drilled in a flat piece of pottery, bone, or gourd shell.

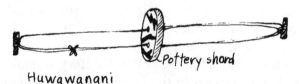

Pottery shard

Huwawanani

You played with this toy by grasping either end of the loop in your hands and twirling the center object over and over until the strings are tightly twisted. Then by pulling and relaxing the ends of the strings, bringing your hands closer together and then pulling them apart, you produced a loud buzzing, humming sound.

Sometimes additional holes were drilled to change the pitch of the sound. Often colorful symbols decorated the early Huwawanani.

Students can make their own buzzing toys using cord and a large button or a wood (or heavy cardboard) disk as the center object. Experiment with shape variations and different placements of the holes on the center disk.

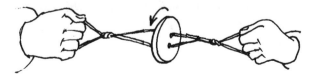

If you are able to use a hand (or electric) drill, try making holes in a thick piece of wood or a flat smooth stone or piece of bone and use one of these as the center object of your Huwawanani.

PEN PALS

This is a good time to initiate pen-pal projects. Bulletin board displays of pictures, appropriate stamps, maps, and photos can stimulate student interest in long-distance correspondence.

A permanent classroom chart might be displayed that recommends the following:

1. When writing pen-pal letters, remember to answer promptly. You'll feel most like writing on the day that you receive the letter from your pen pal.
2. White legibly. You have to keep in mind that your penmanship will be unfamiliar to your pen pal.
3. Tell all about yourself. Tell about your family, friends, school, home, hobbies, pets, favorite books, sports. Be careful not to sound as if you're boasting; be sincere about what you write, and be polite.
4. Don't use slang. Kids from other places often may not be familiar with slang you use at your school.
5. Avoid controversial subjects. Don't talk about things that might make your pen pal uncomfortable; for example, comparisons of religions or political views.
6. Think about things you'd like to exchange—photos, pins, slides, drawings, seashells, tapes, postcards.
7. Learn your pen pal's birthday. Be sure to send him or her a card or small gift.

On the day of the actual letter writing, go over the above list with your students. Ask if they have any questions. (You might pass out sheets of leading question suggestions to help the students with these first letters.)

Below are the names and addresses of elementary schools affiliated with various Native American pueblos or groups in the Southwest. Drop a note to the principal asking to be referred to a teacher whose class of your grade level wants to exchange letters with your group. If you enclose a self-addressed and stamped envelope, this will be appreciated and may speed up the response.

When this mutual letter-writing goes smoothly, it is very exciting and rewarding for all the children involved!

A Word of Caution: It is not always easy to set up a smooth-running exchange of pen-pal letters. Contact one or two of the sources below and enclose a self-addressed, self-stamped envelope for the administrator's convenience. State your grade level, the number of students who will participate (and any specific educational information or any special requests you may have). Wait to receive a positive response to your inquiry before you have the children write their letters. This will save time in the long run and should help guarantee you a successful pen-pal exchange program!

(Navajo) To Hajiilee School
Box 438
Laguna, NM 87026
Attn: Mr. Jim Byrnes, Principal

(Navajo) Ganado Primary School
P.O. Box 1757
Ganado, AZ 86505
Attn: Mr. Sigmund A. Boloz

(Pueblo) Santa Clara Day School
P.O. Box HHH
Española, NM 87532
Attn: Ms. Mil Naranjo

(Pueblo) Santo Domingo School
P.O. Box 640
Bernalillo, NM 87004
Attn: Ms. Judy Duval, Principal

(Pueblo) Jemez Valley Elementary School
8501 Highway 4
Jemez Pueblo, NM 87024
Attn: Teacher of the ____ (Grade level you desire)

INDIVIDUAL HAND-SIZED STUDENT TIMELINES

Here is an excellent way to reinforce historical information you want your class to remember. This technique also aids sequential thinking and is a very good mnemonic device.

You will need: 5″ x 8″ file cards (three for each student), a rubber band for each student, paper cutter, rulers, pencils, 1-inch wide cellophane tape, markers/crayons, glue, scissors, wildlife magazines, and several table knives.

Preparing the Blank Timelines

Mark each file card lengthwise at 2 5/8″ intervals at top and bottom.

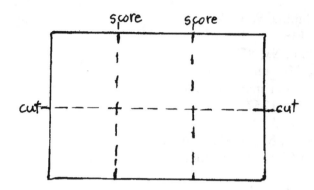

Now use a ruler and the back of the blade of a table knife to connect the first two marks top and bottom; this will score the file card so that it may later be neatly folded. Connect the second set of two marks with a score line also.

Carefully cut each file card in half horizontally. (Each card will now be two 2 1/2″ x 8″ strips.)

Using the Blank Timelines

Demonstrate how to neatly tape two strips (six sections) of a timeline together. Each student tapes two strips together to form the beginning of their individual timeline.

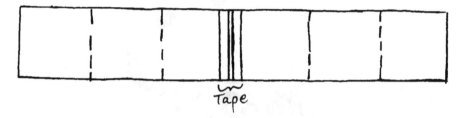

Have each student design an appropriate title section (cover) for their timeline using the words and dates *Native Americans in the Southwest (23,000 B.C. to A.D. 1300)*. Each prints his or her name neatly in tiny letters somewhere on the front and puts a rubber band around it. Collect these blank timelines and return them to the students once you have studied: (1) 23,000–11,000 B.C.: Siberians cross Bering Straits into North America. Each will make a drawing (on the empty page next to their title section) to illustrate the Siberians coming over to North America, and note the date.* Collect the timelines and return them to the students after you have studied: (2) 9,000–5,000 B.C. Prehistoric big game animals become extinct. Children each make a picture with magazine cutouts and/or drawings to illustrate the death of big game in North America. Continue this procedure after the introduction of each important historical date(s). When five dates have been illustrated, each student will tape two more blank strips of six sections to the first timeline sections.

*Students may also show the Native American emergence theory: the first people coming up out of the sipapu.

Before adding (a) new date(s) to the timelines, have the class quickly read through the dates that have been noted to this point on the timelines. Repeating the dates, starting with 23,000 B.C. each time a new date is added, will offer good oral review and will help cement the sequential dates in their minds.

Collect the timelines after new addition(s) are made and keep them in a specific place. This protects the timelines and keeps the images fresh for the students.

When the timelines covering 23,000 B.C. to A.D. 1,300 are completed, neatly display them (in the hallway) at the children's eye-level (using straight pins (not staples or tape, both of which would damage the timelines). (This will encourage the students to review the dates.)

Dates that may be used in a timeline of early Native Americans of the Southwest, 23,000 B.C.–A.D. 13,000:

c. 23,000 B.C.	The first people come to North America; they use the Bering Strait land bridge from Asia to cross over. (Sipapu ermergence)
6000–12,000 B.C.	The first people come to the Southwest area; these are prehistoric big game (mammoth) hunters.
4000 B.C.	Nomadic people roam throughout North America looking for food, meat, and edible plants. They use flint spears, "arrowheads," and fire!
300 B.C.–A.D. 1300	MOGOLLON Culture
c. 300 B.C.	Mogollon make pottery.
c. A.D. 700	Mogollon begin to trade with Hohokam.
c. A.D. 500–200	Peak of Mogollon Culture: irrigation, fine pottery.
A.D. 1250 or 1300	Mogollon are absorbed by the Anasazi.
c. 100 B.C.–A.D. 1500	HOHOKAM Culture
c. A.D. 1100	Hohokam build large irrigation channels and make colorful pots; invent shell etching.
A.D. 1500	Hohokam leave their villages in small bands and disappear.
c. 100 B.C.–A.D. 1300	ANASAZI (Ancestral Puebloan) Culture
c. 100 B.C.	Basketmaker period: they farm and develop weaving; make woven sandals, nets, and traps.
A.D. 500 700	Anasazi develop coiled pottery.
A.D. 650	The bow and arrow are developed.
A.D. 750	Anasazi make adobe and stone buildings.
A.D. 1030	Cliff dweller period: they make complex pueblos of many stories and up to 800 rooms!

A.D. 1130	Pueblo Bonito
A.D. 1000	Raiding bands of Navajo Apaches come into the Southwest.
A.D. 1030–1300	Golden Age of the Anasazi: efficient farming, well-run trade routes. (A.D. 1276–1299 Drought in Southwest.)

Continuing the Timeline

Depending on the time you have, and the emphasis you want to give the 16th through 19th centuries, you may choose to have the children make a large classroom timeline: Native Americans in the Southwest A.D. 1300 to . . .

A.D. 1300	Anasazi leave their cliff houses and disperse. (1492, Columbus comes to this continent; 1519, Cortez invades Mexico and destroys the Aztec Indian Culture.)
A.D. 1540	Coronado and Esteban and Spanish troops explore the Southwest and meet Native peoples; probably the Plains Apaches.
A.D. 1598	Oñate settles the present-day San Juan Pueblo. New Mexico Europeans bring Christian religion, disease and enslavement to Native peoples.
A.D. 1680	Pueblo Revolt: Native people defeat Spanish and force them out of the Southwest.
A.D. 1693	The bloody re-conquest under De Vargas.
A.D. 1700s	Spanish and Pueblo people coexist but times are difficult for all.
A.D. 1846–1848	Mexico loses war with U.S.A. and surrenders New Mexico, Utah, Colorado (and California) to U.S.A. in return for $15 million. This is called The Gadsden Purchase (1853).
A.D. 1850	Pueblo population is at its lowest in the 19th century.
A.D. 1862–1864	The U.S. Government rounds up the Navajo and raiding bands of Native Americans and march them 350 miles to Bosque Redondo Reservation near Pecos, New Mexico.
A.D. 1876	The U.S. Government removes the Chiricahua Apaches from Southeast Arizona to the dry bottomlands of the San Carlos Reservation in Arizona.
A.D. 1888	Geronimo is forced to surrender and all the Chiricahuas are imprisoned by the U.S. government—first in Florida, then in Alabama—and finally are placed on a reservation in Oklahoma.

CREATIVE WRITING (OR JOURNAL-ENTRY) SUGGESTIONS

Here are twelve ideas to help your students begin creative-writing stories or to use as entries in a personal journal.

1. Imagine yourself as one of the first Asians who crosses the Bering Straits into North America. Name several things you see on your long walk. What are you thinking? hoping? Why would it be a better life for you in this new land?

2. Before the early Native Americans went hunting, they probably said a prayer to help bring them good fortune while they were out looking for game. Write a hunting prayer. Tell what kind of animal you need to find. Tell why you need to kill it and how you will show your gratitude.

3. Choose a (four different) food(s) that early Pueblo Indians ate and then write a short blank verse poem about it (each) of these. You can mention the color, texture, smell, taste, or any other impression you may have. Then make a large outline drawing of the (each) food and print or write the poem to fit within it (them). Finally, carefully cut out the shape(s).

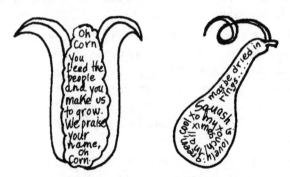

4. Imagine you are a prehistoric architect. Write out the step-by-step directions for building a hogan, a ramada, a pit house, or pueblo apartment. Make these instructions **VERY** complete so that someone reading them could actually use them to construct such a building. (If you like, you can make a comic strip to illustrate each of the steps involved in the building.)

5. Imagine yourself as a red-tailed hawk soaring over the mesas of Arizona. As this hawk, "you" happen to be around one day when an early Native American is busy making a tool (an axe, atl-atl, digging stick, sifting basket—you decide on the kind of tool). Don't tell the name of the tool being made; instead, describe the materials used in making it and the steps "you" (as the hawk) see taken as the unknown object is being created. Try to guess what the human is doing and **WHY**. Remember: Write all of this from the viewpoint of the hawk . . . have fun!

6. Pretend you are a young child late at night watching the signal fires along the trade route to your pueblo. What feelings do you have? Tell what trade goods you and your family want. What does your family have to give in return? How and where do you get these things? Finally, write about meeting and talking to the runner/trader. Tell what you say and ask him—and what he tells you.

7. It takes about a dozen steps for a Native American to create a pottery bowl: dig clay, crumble it, moisten it, put it through a screen to remove rocks, roll coils, form pot, scrape it, dry it, paint it with a slip, add design, and fire pot. Write a make-believe diary as if you are a Pueblo potter. Write an entry for each day you are involved in these steps to make a piece of pottery. Use lots of details. Tell what kind of weather you have on each day. Tell what you're thinking. Show the shape you make and the design. Does your pot fire successfully? What do you do with it?

8. Pretend you are a young Zuni Indian man who will be married tomorrow. You will soon be going to live with your new wife's family. Tell the different ways that this will change your life. Why will it be okay with you to do this? Explain how you are feeling about your parents, about your wife to be, and about being a married man!

9. Read (or listen to) the Southwestern Native American riddles. Then choose a (five different) thing(s) in nature and make up a clever riddle to describe it (each of them). Have fun trying out each of your riddles on someone. Which is your best riddle? Why does it work so well? (Now choose a [five] thing[s] made by early people in the Southwest. Write a riddle to describe it [each of these].)

10. Write a song or poem or prayer to say how much you and your people need and want rain. Tell several ways that rain can help you all. Say why you think you deserve a good rainfall. Remember that you are asking all this as a *favor*, so be sure to sound pleading and appreciative.

11. In America, getting your driver's license is one way of marking the change in your life from being a kid to being a grown-up. (Think of some other ways we in the United States mark going from being a child to becoming an adult. What do these ways of marking change have in common?) List five or six times in your life that you feel marked a real change in your growing up. Now write a sentence or two about how you were made to feel and what you were thinking on each of these five or six occasions.

12. Imagine yourself, *if you are a girl*, as the young person "becoming" Changing Woman. Write about your thoughts and feelings on each of the days of the ceremony. Tell how it feels to become Changing Woman herself! *If you are a boy*, imagine you are one of the Gan, the Mountain Spirit dancers who come out each night to take part in the Changing Woman ceremony. Tell what you think as you dance around the fire. Write about the young girl in the festivities: How does she look? What do you think of her? Do you like her—why (not)? What do you think of this Changing Woman ceremony?

CULMINATING ACTIVITY: CREATING A "MUSEUM OF THE DESERT INDIANS" (OR A "MUSEUM OF SOUTHWESTERN ANTHROPOLOGY")

When your (older) students have completed their studies of Native Americans of the Southwest, discuss with them how you might share with others the things you've made and learned these last weeks.

If the idea of constructing a classroom museum appeals to the group, start off by making a class-generated list defining a museum and the many things you may find in one (displays, signs, glass cases; examples of art, clothing, religious items, and so on). Then have them list all the things they made during their studies (tools, food, weaving, pottery, toys, fetishes, timeline, etc.). Help them decide how they might best exhibit these. Finally, organize committees to each take responsibility for a specific aspect of your museum. This might involve categories such as large signs, labels for exhibits, display of shelters, crafts, a large timeline, etc.; let students come up with the specific categories. Then ask for volunteers for each category (committee) and let these children organize themselves to target tasks to be done and how best to effectively complete them. Each committee should make a list of materials they will need to facilitate their work and construct the museum displays. See that the materials are provided.

If at all possible the students should visit a local museum and keep a list of all the physical elements of a "good museum"; e.g., well-written labels and signs, intriguing objects, a clear chronology, thought-provoking exhibits, a few unexpected (i.e., hands-on) displays, and so on.

When their museum is complete, invite "the public" and open the doors!

OTHER SUGGESTIONS FOR CULMINATING ACTIVITIES

Have the students each write about the following:

1. A time capsule is a container made to hold and protect important things from a historic time culture. It is then buried or put into a vault until a much later time (even centuries later) when it is opened and its contents are studied. Time capsules originated in the 20th century, but if you had lived in A.D. 800 and you were told to collect things from that time to be placed in a large jar and hidden in a cave for future humans to study. . . . What things would you have chosen? Make a list of objects that best represent one of the three earliest cultures of the Southwest. Be sure to include examples of food, clothing, tools, children, art, crafts, religion, trade, and so on. (You can make an X-ray drawing of the filled jar, as if you could see through it and could see all of the objects in the jar.)

2. At the end of their Native American studies, the students will each list *Five Things I Didn't Know* before they studied the Native Americans of the Southwest.

    As the unit progresses, you could tell your class, "At the end of our Native American Studies, I'll want you each to tell me one thing you still don't know, but would like to have learned about." This exercise will help the children see that these studies—and learning itself—continue even though "a unit of study" may be completed. It also will help you see where these students' areas of personal interest lie—and may help you in planning the "Desert Native Americans" unit . . . for next year!

Notes for "Activities for the Classroom":

1. As the Native American reviewer of these materials pointed out: "This activity is not appropriate for use with young Native Americans here in the Southwest, as they understand that in their culture only elders are allowed to make Cradle Kachinas. So if you, the teacher, ask them to construct such little toys, these students would be made to feel very ambivalent."

2. A good source book for Cradle Kachinas is *Hopi Kachina Dolls* by Oscar Branson (Tucson, AZ: Treasure Chest Publications, 1993).

THE DESERT INDIANS

Ready-to-Use
Reproducible Activities

HOW THE FIRST PEOPLE CAME HERE

This is a picture of the land we live in: North America. Long, long ago no people lived here. Ice covered much of the land. This ice made a land-bridge so people could cross over to our land.

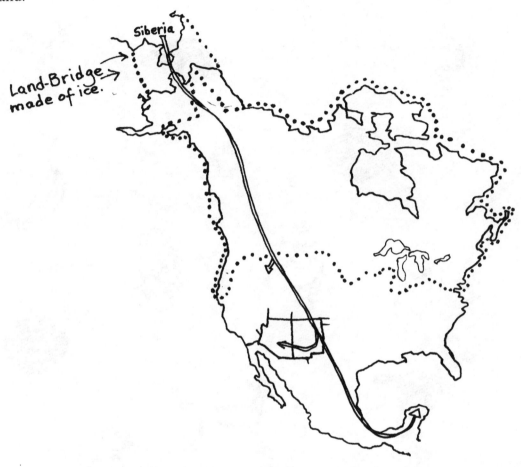

Many scientists believe that the first people came here from Siberia. Many Native Americans do not believe this. Their old songs and stories say that the first people came up out of the sipapu (see-pah-poo´), the center of the earth. This is what they believe.

Directions:

1. Use a white crayon to cover all the places the ice covered. This is marked with

2. (Ask your teacher to help you.) Find where you live in North America. Mark it with a

3. Outline the southwestern part of our land with green. This is the states of Arizona, New Mexico, and parts of Colorado, Utah, Texas and Nevada.

4. Make a long orange arrow to show where scientists think people came from Siberia, through Canada, down to the Southwest.

CAN YOU FIND THE TWINS?

Draw a line between each pair of twins. Then you can color all the twins—if you have time.

A SOUTHWESTERN PIT HOUSE

The first people in the southwest desert made their stick and grass houses in holes or pits.

This kept them cool. Draw a pit house in the Then show the desert all around it.

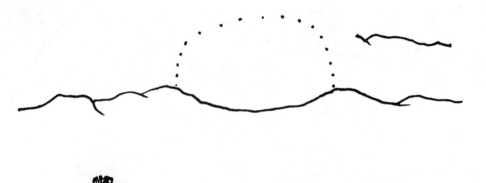

Draw bushes, 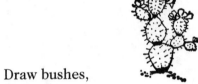 , rabbits,  , and
Color them too.

AN EARLY BOWL

1,000 years ago, some of the first people in the Southwest made bowls with animal pictures on them. Here are a few animal designs.

Just like THEY did!

Think of a good animal picture. Draw it in this bowl. Make it BIG. Use just black, grey, and white to color it.

© 1995 by The Center for Applied Research in Education

Name _____

COUNT US!

Write the number of each kind of
thing in the ◯ next to it.

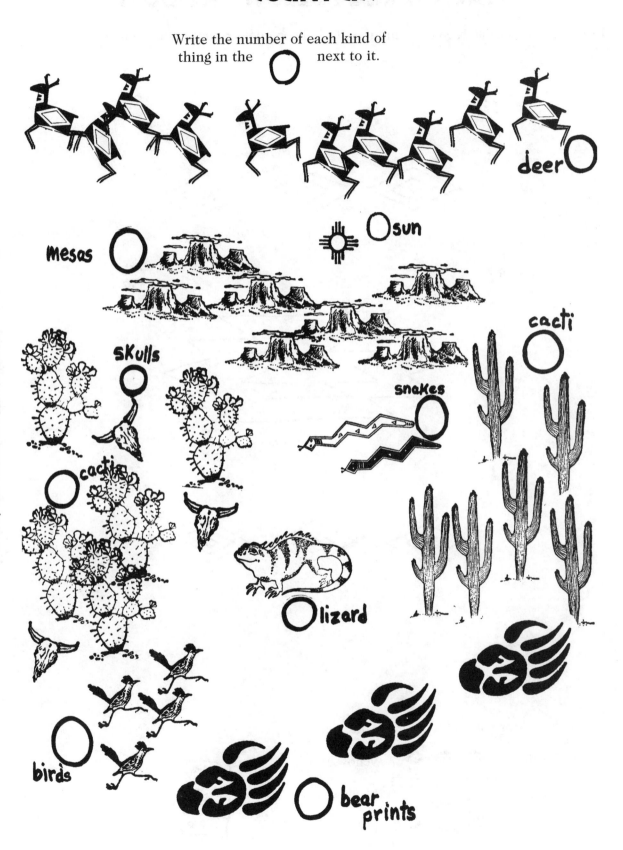

deer ◯

◯ sun

Mesas ◯

cacti ◯

Skulls ◯

snakes ◯

◯ cacti

◯ lizard

◯ birds

◯ bear prints

Name _____

NAVAJO RUG FOLLOW-THE-DOTS

Use a pencil. Start at 1, go to 2, and then to 3. Keep on going until you get to 13!

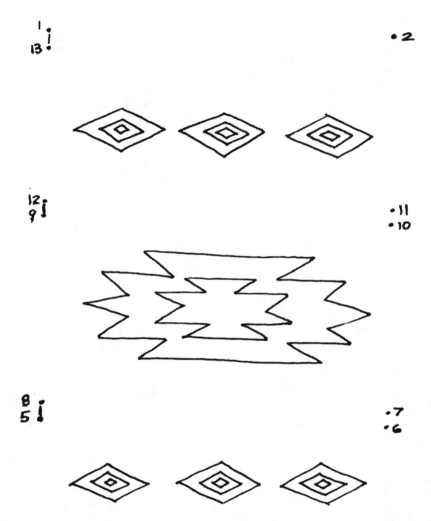

Then:
   Make a fringe at each corner of your rug.

   Color the ◇ ◇ ◇ yellow.

   Color the ▭ black.

   Color the ◈ red.

THE PIMA BASKET MAZE

A maze is a long hidden path. This is a basket that was made long ago by the Pima Indians and it has a maze woven into it. Use a pencil to show the little man how to go into the maze and get at last to the middle of the basket. Good luck!

Start here.

CRADLE KACHINAS

Hopi babies play with little Cradle Kachina dolls. Some of them look like this one, which is a Mudhead.

If you have 3 little fluffy feathers (from a pillow), you can glue them to my head and ears.

Color the head and ears brown.

Color the left arm, hand and right shoulder yellow.

Color the right hand, arm and left shoulder green.

Color the 3 bottom strips red.

RAMADA

Cut out this pattern on thick solid line fold it along dotted lines and glue it as shown to make a ramada, the summer arbor of the Pima and Papago Indians.

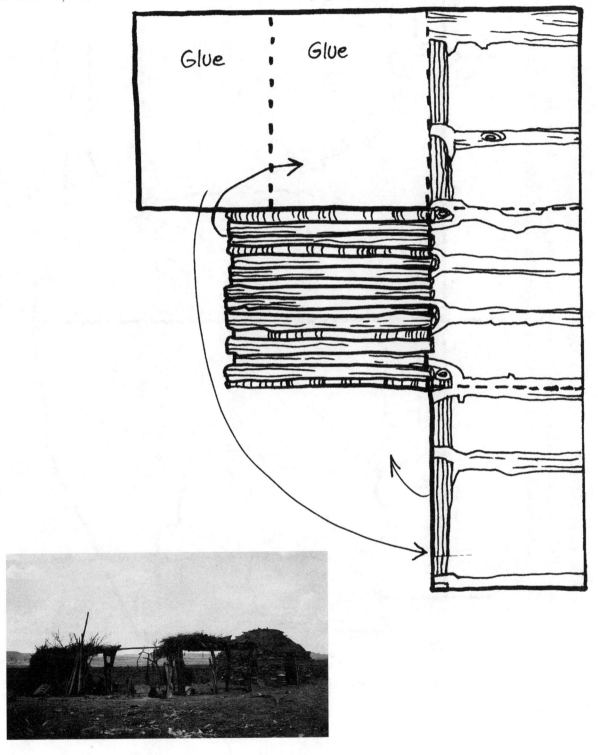

Glue   Glue

Photo 45. Navajo summer and winter hogans; circa 1920. *Courtesy Museum of New Mexico (neg. no 68762).*

See page 167 for lower grade recipe.

A MAP OF THE SOUTHWEST

1. Fill in these states: Arizona, Texas, Colorado, Utah, New Mexico.
2. Fill in these rivers' names: Colorado, Gila, Little Colorado, Santa Cruz, Rio Grande, Salt River, San Juan, San Pedro, Verde.
3. Fill in these place and mountain names: Hopi Mesas, Mesa Verde, Zuni, Rio Grande Pueblos, Mogollon, Mimbres.

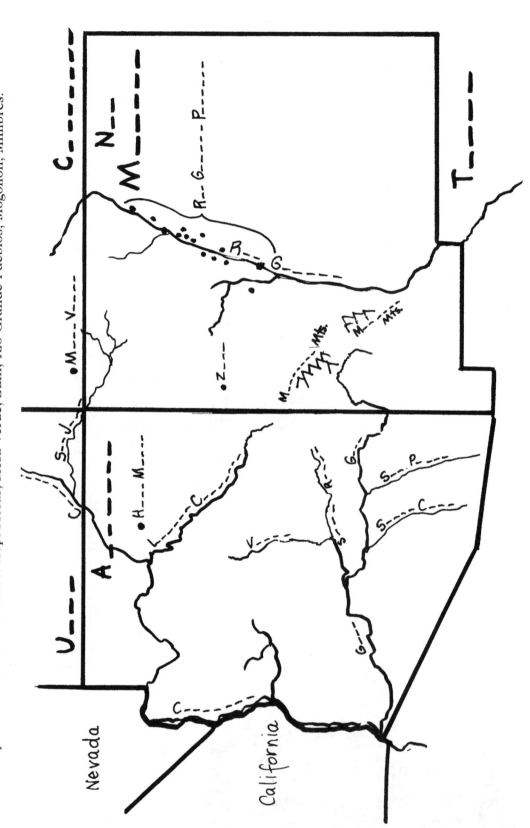

EARLY SOUTHWESTERN NATIVE AMERICAN GIRLS' CLOTHING

Carefully color and cut these out. Have fun playing with your paper doll.

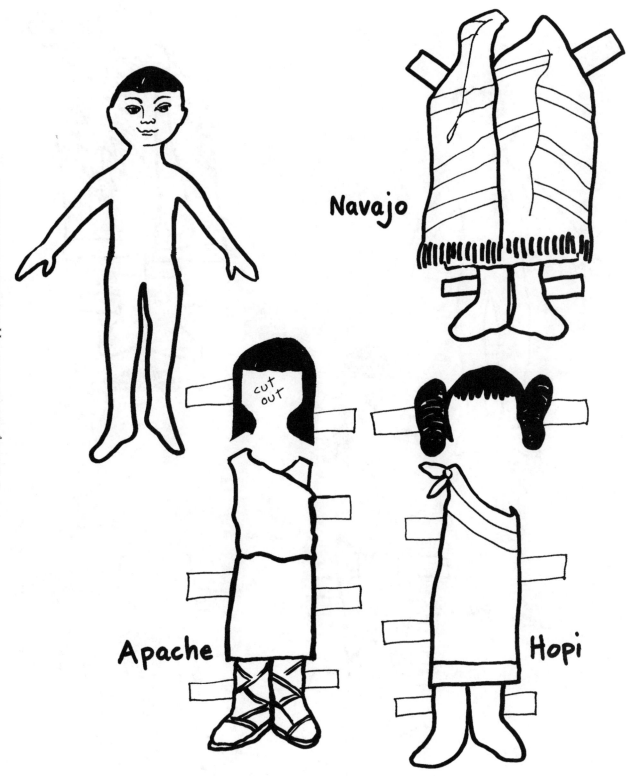

Navajo

Apache

Hopi

EARLY SOUTHWESTERN
NATIVE AMERICAN BOYS' CLOTHING

Carefully color and cut out this paper doll and his clothes. Get together with friends and make up a little play using your paper dolls.

Navajo

Chongo: at back of head.

cut out

Apache

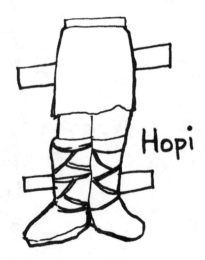

Hopi

134

THE PIMA AND PAPAGO KI

Use watercolors or crayons to color the horizontal sticks dark brown, and the vertical grasses light green. Cut along the heavy outside lines. Fold down on the dotted lines. Apply glue to the place marked Glue 1. Swing 2 over onto 1 and glue down. Swing 3 onto 1 and glue down. Apply glue to 3 and 4. Glue these under 5. Apply glue to 6 and 7. Swing 7 on top of 6 and 6 on top of 2. Finally bring the left edge of the Ki over onto 7 and glue down. Your Ki is complete!

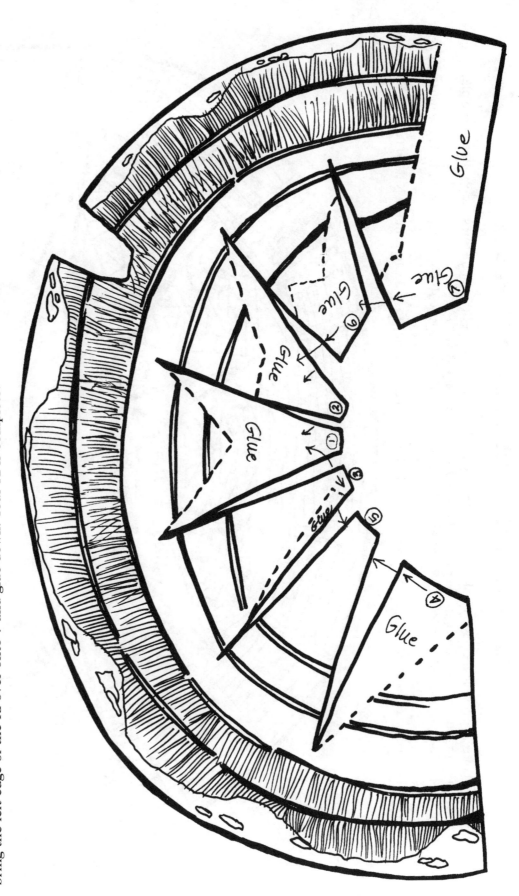

135

HOGAN: A SIX-SIDED NAVAJO HOUSE

Use crayons to color in every log. Do <u>NOT</u> color where it says "Glue." Cut along the solid outside lines. Apply glue to the place where it says 1. Then swing the part to the right over onto the glued 1 part. Let glue dry.

Then apply glue to 2, swing 1 over onto glued part. Let dry. Repeat these steps with 3—5 until, with 6, you will finish your Navajo Hogan!

Think of how you can use your hogan (with brush, sand, sheep) (in a diorama) to show how many Navajo families live there.

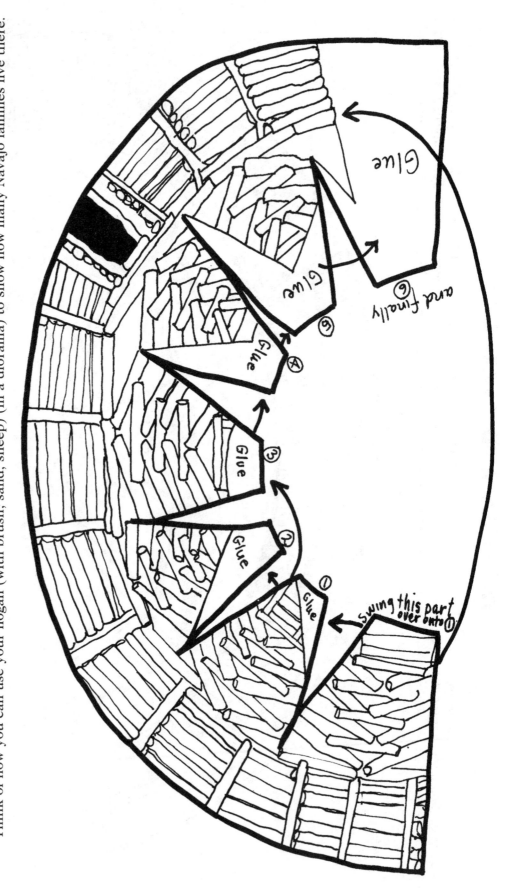

AN ANIMAL HELPER

Start at 1. Draw a line to 2 and then to 3 and so on—until you get to 60! This is a bear animal helper.

The 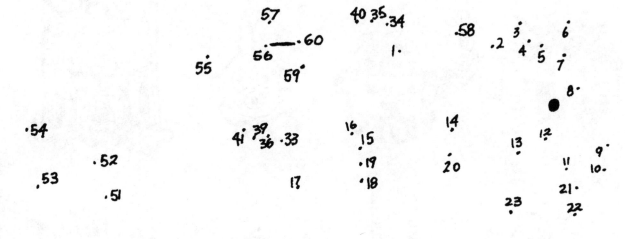 on his back was to help you hunt well.

The is the life (breath) line of the bear.

1. Color red.

2. Color green.

3. The is tied on the back of the bear.

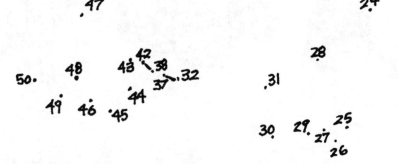

Draw two little feathers under the string too.

4. Color the string brown.

5. Then carefully color the bear animal helper black.

KACHINAS

Here are the faces of 14 different Kachinas. Look at their names in the lists below. Match each Kachina with its name. Print its English name under each face.

Hopi
Nangasohu
Sohu
Patuna
Koshare
Matya
Poli Sio
Sowi-ing
Soyoko
Tawa
To Cha
Koyemsi
Pohaha
Hahai-Wuhti
Saistastana

English
Chasing Star
Horned Owl
Squash Kachina
Clown
Hand Kachina
Butterfly Kachina
Deer Kachina
Ogre Woman
Sun Kachina
Hummingbird
Mudhead
Horned Kachina
Kachina Mother
Rain Priest
  of the North

BUTTERFLY DANCERS, PAGE 1

These two girls are Butterfly Dancers. They were drawn by a Hopi artist 100 years ago. The little man is meant to look as if he were in front of the two girls. He holds a tall flag to show how much his people love their corn crops.

Use watercolors or crayons to color this picture with the same colors that the Hopi artist used. You will need: red, yellow, pale green, blue, black, white, and tan. (See page 2 for exact directions.)

BUTTERFLY DANCERS,
PAGE 2

Color your picture in this way:

RED: Cheeks; belts; right-hand stripe on corn flag (banner); the **outline** of each tablita (worn on head), and the **outlines** of the designs on the tablitas ; scarf on man's head.

YELLOW: Bracelets; foot wrappings; left dancer's cape; bottom stripe on right-hand dancer's cape; the middle of the on the right-hand dancer's tablita.

PALE GREEN: Tablitas; bottom stripe on dresses; the little pine branch in each girl's hands.

BLUE: Right-hand dancer's cape; the bottom stripe on the other dancer's cape; on left tablita; outline of on right tablita.

BLACK: The hair of all three people; the dresses; the man's leggings; the middle stripe on the corn banner; the outline of the ◇ on the right-hand belt.

WHITE: The two girls' faces; the left-hand stripe on the corn banner; the necklaces; the center of the ; the edges of and ; the ties on the capes; the tiny feathers at the tops of the tablitas.

TAN: The dancers' arms, necks, legs, toes; the man's whole body.

© 1995 by The Center for Applied Research in Education

A SYMBOL STORY, PAGE 1

A symbol is a little picture that stands for something in the world. On page 2 are 27 symbols that early Southwestern people used.

Fill in the name below each little picture. (Sometimes their may be two different symbols for the same word. . . . <u>why</u> do you think this could happen?)

Then read the story-starter below and use a SYMBOL (not a word) to fill in each blank. Remember: There are <u>many</u> different ways to fill in the blanks and complete this tale . . . but, of course, it should make sense!

It was a warm day. Then a   covered the

        . Three   came into the sky,

and   flashed.   began to fall. A

           flew over the   and dropped one of

his   . Then a   came out of the for-

est and left his   in the mud. A tall

            came down to the   with a   in

his hand. He tried to hit a   but he missed.

The   stopped and a   came

into the sky. The   saw some   .

They looked up at a big green   and they all yelled,

"DADDY! DADDY!"

A   sat on a   and sucked

out some honey. At last the   went down. . . . The

            came up. There was only one   in

the sky. A   passed by.

A SYMBOL STORY, PAGE 2

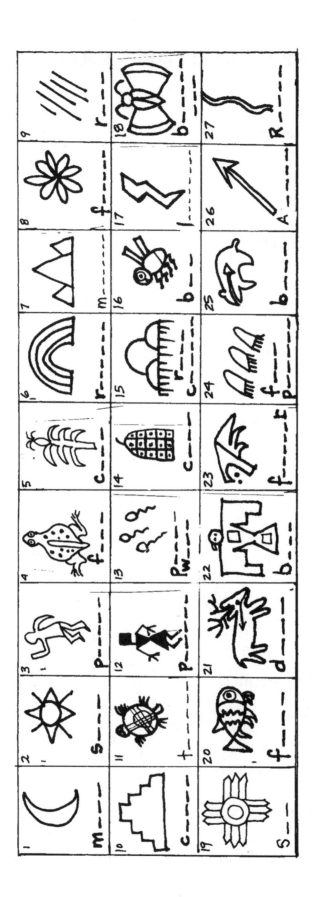

PUEBLO INDIAN COOKIES

(called Biscochitas* by the Spanish)

6 cups unbleached flour

3 tsp. baking powder

1 tsp. salt

2 cups lard (buy this from an organic meat market, if possible)

3 tsp. anise seed; bruised in a mortar

1/4 cup orange juice

1/2 cup sugar

2 eggs

1. Wash your hands.

2. Sift together: flour, salt and baking powder.

3. Cream lard and sugar in a second bowl. Then add the flour mixture to the lard mixture.

4. Now mix together: the anise seeds and the 2 eggs. Stir them until the eggs are fluffy. Add these to the flour mixture.

5. Add orange juice, little by little, until the dough holds together. The dough should be firm like biscuit dough.

6. Heat the oven to 400°.

7. Roll out the dough to 1/4″ thickness. Cut into small shapes with cookie cutters or a table knife. Place on a cookie sheet.

8. Sprinkle the tops of the cookies with a mixture of 1/4 cup sugar and 1 T. cinnamon.

9. Bake 10 - 15 minutes.

¡ Buen provecho! (ENJOY!)

© 1995 by The Center for Applied Research in Education

Photo 46. Pueblo Indian bread; circa 1889. *Credit unknown.*

*Say: bees-koh-cheé-tohs: it means "little biscuits."

143

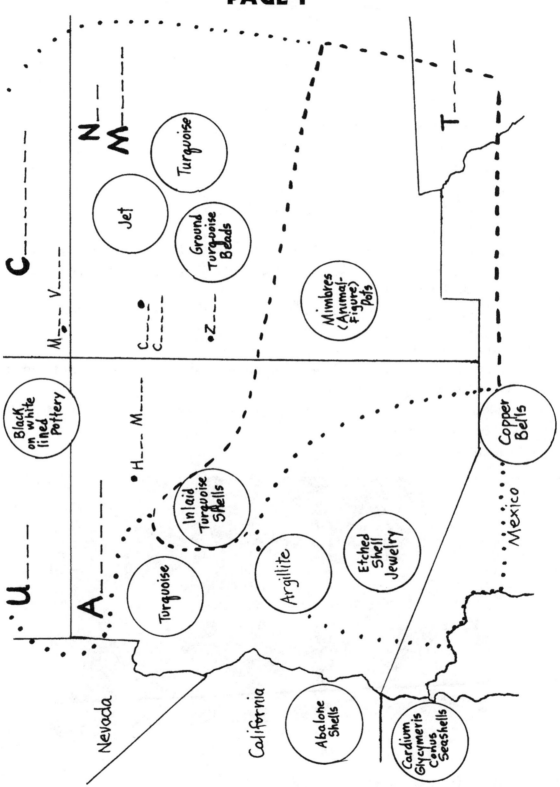

EARLY CULTURES OF THE SOUTHWEST, PAGE 1

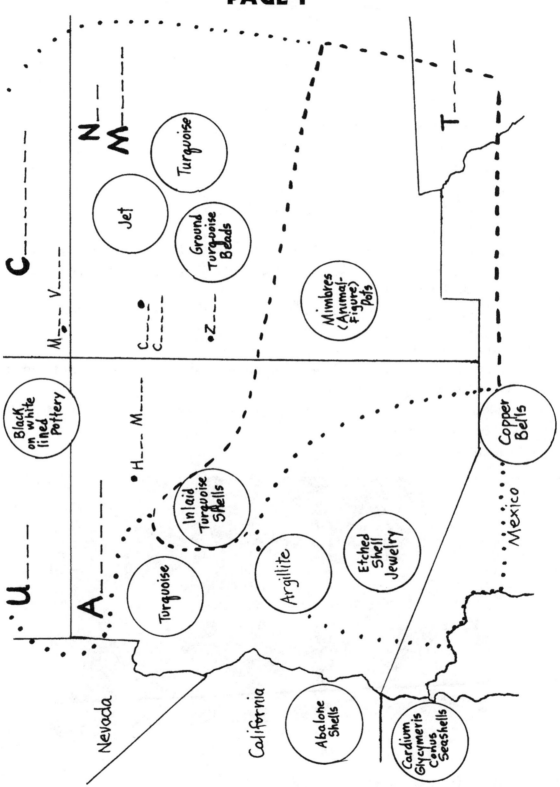

Turquoise

Jet

Ground Turquoise Beads

Mimbres (Animal-Figure) Pots

Black on white lined Pottery

Copper Bells

Inlaid Turquoise Shells

Turquoise

Argillite

Etched Shell Jewelry

México

Nevada

California

Abalone Shells

Cardium Glycymeris Conus Seashells

*How a people act and the things they make become their culture.

EARLY CULTURES OF THE SOUTHWEST, PAGE 2

The three early cultures of the Southwest were the Mogollon, the Hohokam, and the Anasazi.

1. Fill in the names of the four southwestern states on whose land these people lived.

2 Outline in red the area where the Mogollon lived (southern New Mexico, eastern Arizona and part of Texas and Mexico). Print MOGOLLON at the top of this area.

3. Outline in orange the area where the Hohokam lived (southern Arizona and part of Mexico). Print HOHOKAM across this area.

4. Use blue to outline where the Anasazi lived (northern Arizona and New Mexico and southern Utah and Colorado.) Print ANASAZI across the middle of this area. Then fill in these important places in the Anasazi area: Mesa Verde, Zuni, Chaco Canyon, Hopi Mesas.

The large circles on page 1 are to show the crafts made by these cultures and where the peoples got the materials from which to make these crafts!

5. Carefully cut out the circles below and find where each belongs on page 1. Glue them in place. (You can also give them the correct colors.)

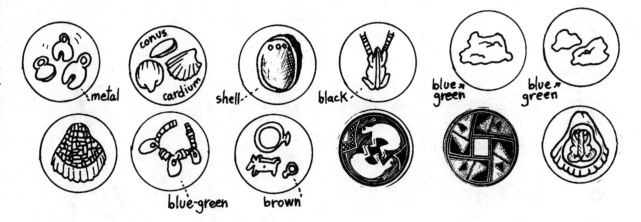

THE GENERAL PLACES WHERE SOUTHWESTERN NATIVE PEOPLE LIVE TODAY

Use yellow to outline the place of the Desert People.
Use brown to outline the place of the Farmers.
Use green to outline the place of the Shepherds.

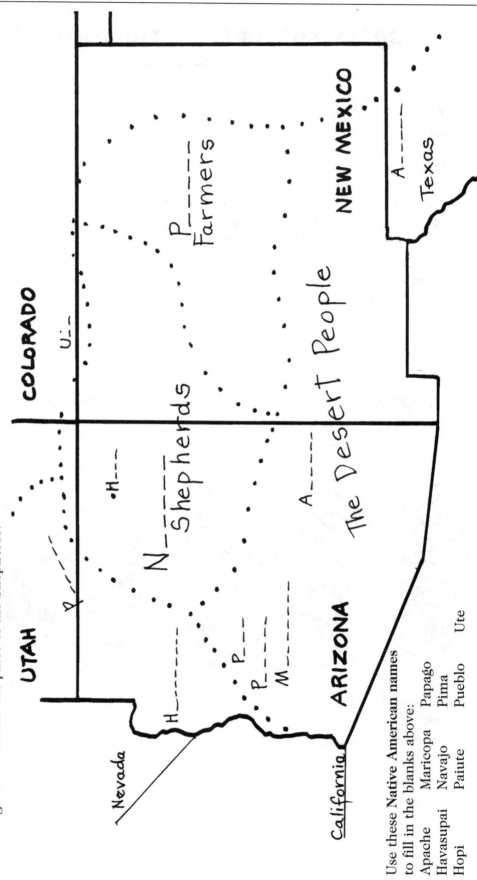

Use these Native American names
to fill in the blanks above:

Apache	Maricopa	Papago
Havasupai	Navajo	Pima
Hopi	Paiute	Pueblo	Ute

THE FIRST 3 CULTURES OF THE SOUTHWEST
DIRECTIONS

The three earliest groups of people in the Southwest were:

> The Mogollon
> The Hohokam
> The Anasazi

Read over the descriptions on page 2 of the different <u>times</u>, <u>food</u>, <u>shelter</u>, and <u>crafts</u> of these people.

Decide which description in each of the four sections belongs to the Mogollon and which to the Hohokam—<u>and</u> which goes with the Anasazi. (For example: the Mogollon were the earliest culture in the Southwest, so their time is 300 B.C. . . .)

Cut out each description along the dotted line . . . and glue it where it belongs on page 1.

Photo 47. 19th-century pottery figures by Pueblo potters. *Courtesy Museum of New Mexico (neg. no. 58852).*

THE FIRST 3 CULTURES OF THE SOUTHWEST, PAGE 1

MOGOLLON Time:_____

Food:_____

Shelter: _____

Crafts: _____

HOHOKAM
Time:_____

Food: _____

Shelter: _____

Crafts: _____

ANASAZI Time:
_____

Food: _____

Shelter: _____

Crafts: _____

THE FIRST 3 CULTURES OF THE SOUTHWEST, PAGE 2

TIME They Lived:

About 300 B.C. to A.D. 1300

About 100 B.C. to A.D. 1500

About 100 B.C. to A.D. 1300

Ways of Getting FOOD:

Farmers with 100s of miles of irrigation ditches; raised big fields of corn, squash, cotton, tobacco, and beans.

These hunter-gatherers became simple farmers.

They hunted with atl-atl and later . They raised red corn, cotton, sunflowers (for seeds). They didn't have big irrigation ditches, but they were very smart when using any available water.

SHELTERS They Made:

Permanent villages of about 30 pit houses and 200 people, each was built by a stream.

Thatched-roof pit houses until A.D. 750, then adobe and stone buildings. In A.D. 1030 cliff cities with adobe apartment buildings of 800 rooms for 1,000 people.

Their main village was lived in for 1500 years; it had 100 pit houses and covered 300 acres.

Their CRAFTS:

They set up great trade routes, began weaving in about 100 B.C. (baskets, cloth, sandals, traps). Complex painted pots painted with grey, black, white. Inlaid mosaic jewelry.

Traders who made beautiful cloth, etched shells, mosaic mirrors.

They made pitch-lined baskets for cooking and undecorated brown pots. In about A.D. 700 they began making Mimbres pots with animal and people figures. Turquoise, shell and bone necklaces and bracelets.

PUEBLO BUILDING
(DIRECTIONS)

First Floor

Use watercolors or crayons to color the walls a rich mud color. (Do not color where it says GLUE.) Cut along solid lines. Fold down on dotted lines. Swing each side part in the direction of the arrow. Apply glue to places marked GLUE. Hold paper in place until glue is dry.

Second Floor

Here again you will color the walls and not color where it says GLUE. Cut along solid lines and fold down on dotted lines. Apply glue to area ①. Swing it under "Glue: second" and hold it in place until glue is dry. Apply glue to area ②. Swing "the top of roof" over glue and hold it in place until this glue is dry. Apply glue to area ③ and area ④ and glue the sides of the building together.

Finally apply glue to the flaps that go under the second floor. Glue this second floor to the top of the first floor building.

Third Floor

Color the walls brown and do not color the parts that say GLUE. Cut along solid lines and fold down on dotted lines. Apply glue to area ① and swing it under the roof. Hold it in place until the glue dries. Glue area ② to the inside of the wall with the strings of chile. Glue area ③ to the inside of the other side of this wall. Now apply glue to the four flaps that fold under this third floor and place this little building inside the dotted box on the second floor roof. Hold it in place until the glue dries.

Color the two buttresses brown both inside and outside and cut out along the solid lines. Fold the flaps in and apply glue. Glue each buttress to one side of the wall to complete your Pueblo Building!

© 1995 by The Center for Applied Research in Education

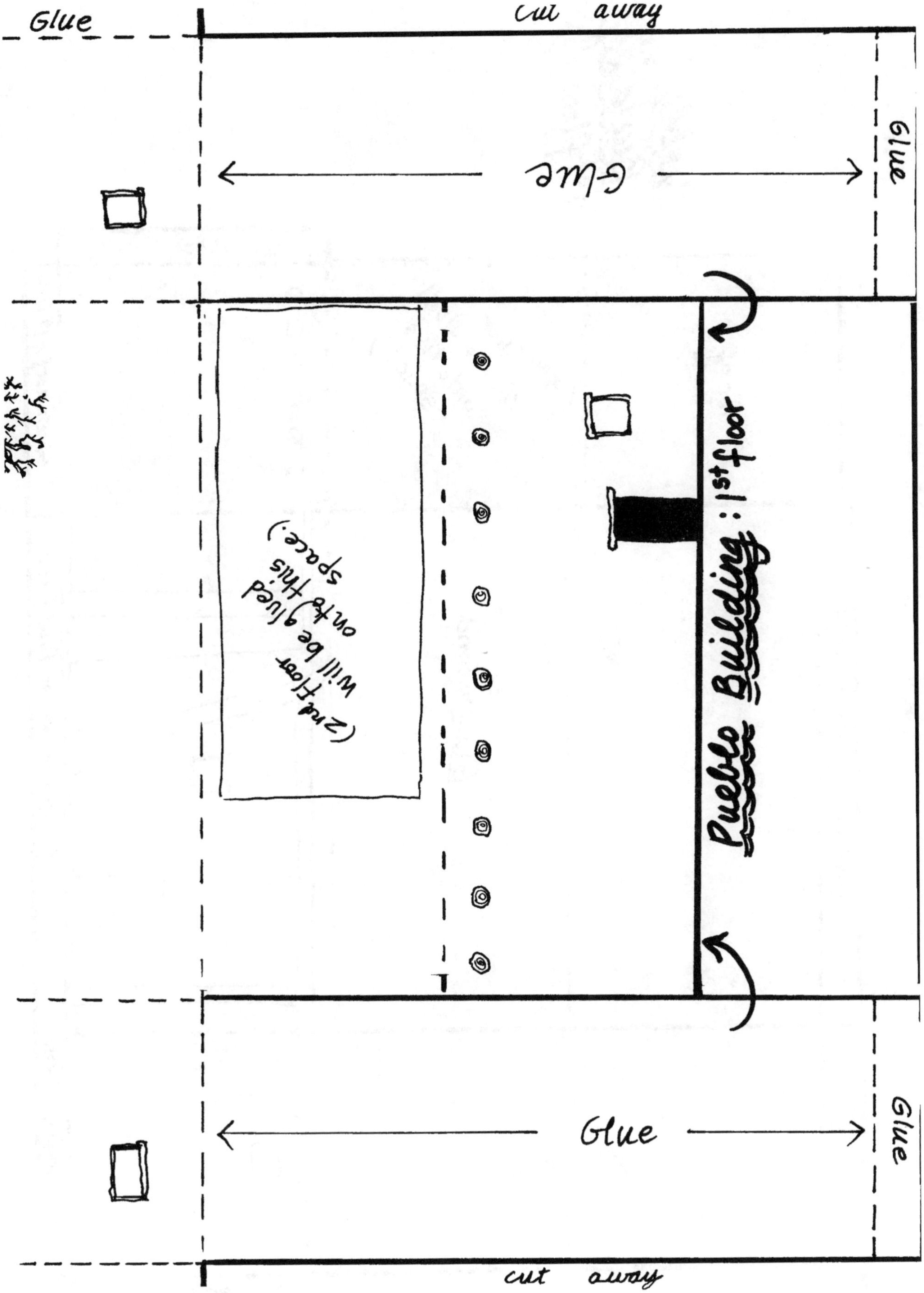

Glue

Glue

cut away

Glue

Pueblo Building : 1st floor

(2nd floor
will be glued
on this
space.)

Glue

Glue

cut away

151

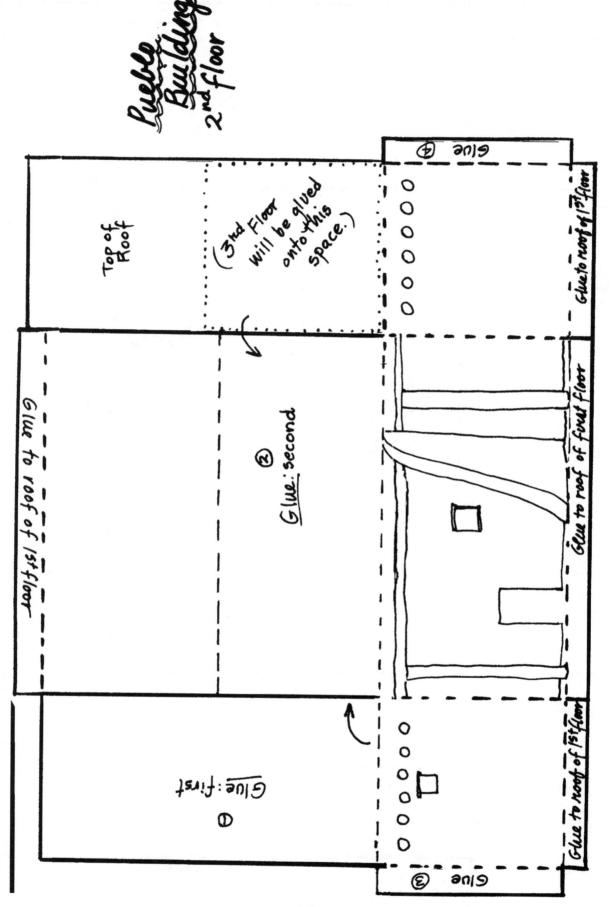

Pueblo Building 2nd Floor

Top of Roof

(3rd Floor will be glued onto this space.)

② Glue: second

Glue to roof of 1st floor

Glue to roof of first floor

Glue to roof of 1st floor

① Glue: first

Glue ③

Glue ④

Glue to roof of 1st floor

Pueblo Building
Third Floor

Finished Pueblo Building

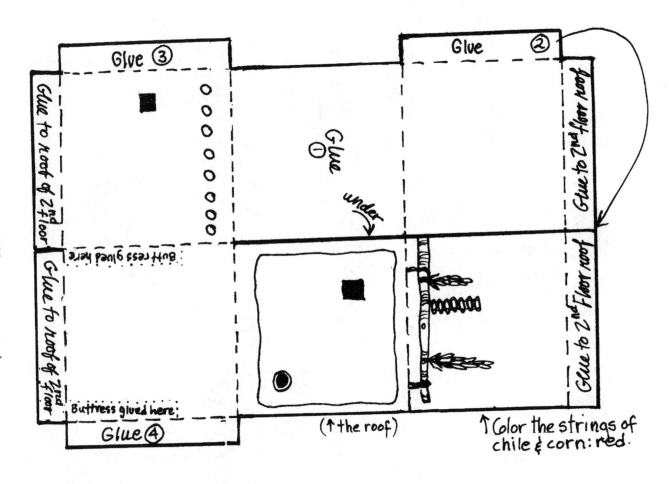

Glue ③

Glue ②

Glue to 2nd floor roof

Glue ①

under

Glue to roof of 2nd floor

Buttress glued here

Glue to roof of 2nd floor

Buttress glued here

Glue ④

Glue to 2nd floor roof

Glue to 2nd floor roof

(↑ the roof)

↑ Color the strings of chile & corn: red.

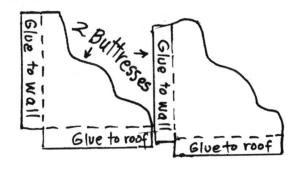

Glue to wall

2 Buttresses

Glue to wall

Glue to roof

Glue to roof

153

A RAIN VESSEL

When you have connected the dots from 1 - 107, you will have an object that the early Pueblo people used for catching and holding water. The ⎍ sides stand for rain clouds. All the pictures on it are water animals asking for rain to fall.

   Use white, black, brown, and rust to color in your rain vessel; these are the colors used by those potters long ago!

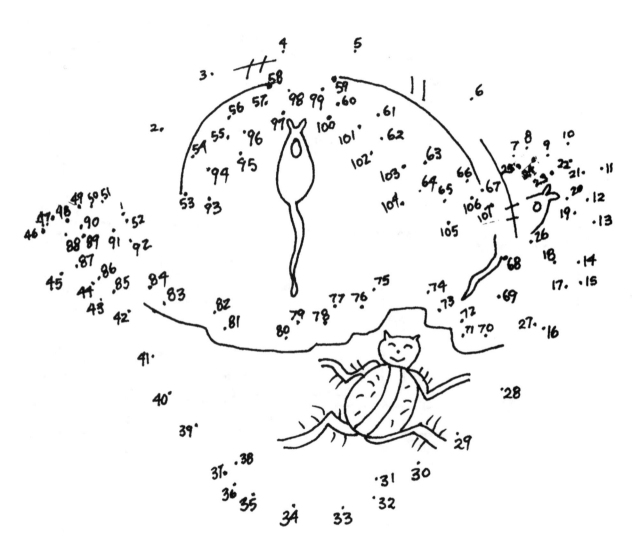

AN EARLY POT

You are an archaeologist. These are some pottery shards* you have found. Cut them out carefully and put them together to form an early Anasazi pot.

Glue your pot carefully to a sheet of paper.

Then you can color in the design, if you'd like. *One piece is missing!

19 PUEBLOS WORD SEARCH

E	U	Q	U	S	E	T	M	R	SAN	J	S	Y	N
P	D	S	T	I	Q	K	D	L	T	U	H	O	P
I	F	E	I	T	S	U	A	N	A	A	T	SAN	F
L	G	X	H	SAN	R	L	J	I	Z	N	I	T	E
E	L	U	C	I	L	D	E	F	O	N	S	O	G
F	M	P	O	J	B	V	N	T	C	H	S	D	B
SAN	T	A	C	L	A	R	A	C	A	J	I	O	E
V	E	Q	U	Y	SAN	☺	M	K	E	X	R	M	U
S	A	N	U	G	A	L	B	M	T	SAN	U	I	Q
B	I	S	M	C	O	P	E	U	A	F	C	N	A
W	D	N	O	L	N	Z	U	N	I	W	I	G	O
H	N	M	D	A	H	I	J	E	Z	G	P	O	J
S	A	N	Z	E	T	C	L	A	U	S	E	A	U

Look in the puzzle above and find these pueblos. Circle each one:

1. Acoma
2. Cochiti
3. Isleta
4. Jemez
5. Laguna
6. Nambe
7. Picuris
8. Pojoaque
9. Sandia
10. San Felipe
11. San Ildefonso
12. San Juan
13. Santa Ana
14. Santa Clara
15. Santo Domingo
16. Taos
17. Tesuque
18. Zia
19. Zuni

They may be written  or  or or . . . ?

Some will even be written backwards. . . .

ANSWER TO 19 PUEBLOS WORD SEARCH

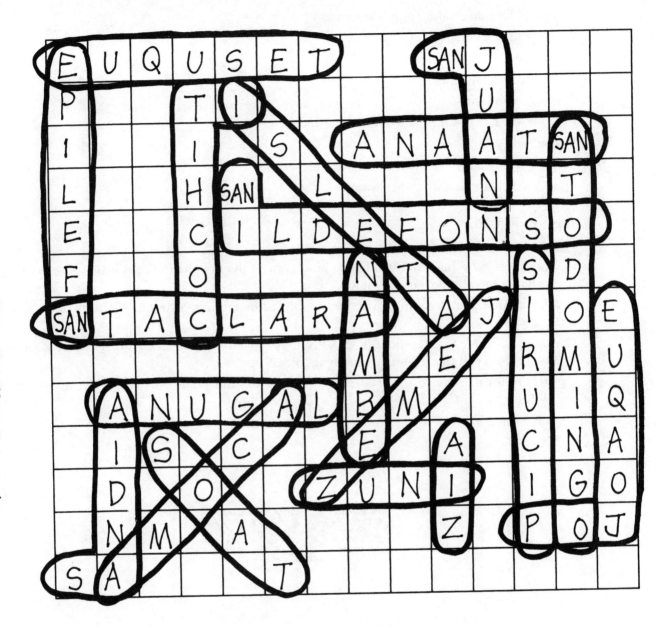

157

NAVAJO FRY-BREAD

4 cups unbleached flour (plus a bit extra)

3 tsp. baking powder

1 tsp. salt

1 1/2 cups warm water

2 T. powdered milk

oil (the Navajos use lard; corn oil is fine too)

honey

electric frying pan, big bowl, tongs, (aprons),

cookie sheets lined with paper towels

1. Wash your hands.
2. Fill the frying pan 1/2 full of oil. Turn pan on to HIGH.
3. Measure the first 5 ingredients into the bowl. Knead the dough, adding a little more flour if you like, until the dough does not stick to your hands.
4. Divide the dough into small balls (the size of golf balls? Experiment.) Flatten each ball until it is thin.
5. Carefully slide one into the hot oil; an adult may have to do this: **ask your teacher**! Cook on both sides until the fry-bread is a light golden brown.
6. Use the tongs to remove the fry-bread from the oil and place each one on the paper towel-lined sheet.
7. Serve warm, "drizzled" with honey. . . . DE-LI-CIOUS!

THE
DESERT INDIANS

Teacher's Resource Guide

RESOURCE LIST

CATALOGS

Dover Publications, Inc.
31 East Second Street
Mineola, NY 11501

> (Reasonably priced American
> Indian books; colored postcards,
> such as "Six Kachina
> Dolls"—request American
> Indian catalog)

Interact
Box 997-Y89
Lakeside, CA 92040

> (Simulations: "Who Really
> Discovered America?" "Mahopa,"
> "Honor"—grades 4-11)

KC Publications
Box 14883
Las Vegas, NV 89114

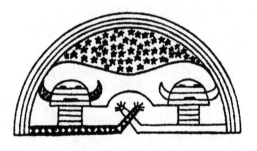

> (Very inexpensive softcover
> books on Southwestern Native
> American cultures)

Navajo Nation Museum
P.O. Box 308, Highway 264
Window Rock, AZ 86515

> (Books; videos; posters;
> children's books)

Rough Rock Press
RRD 5, Box 217
Chinle, AZ 86503

> (Pictorial history of
> Navajos; teaching guide
> for Indian literature;
> Coyote stories; and so on)

BOOKS

Cobblestone Publishers, Inc.
7 School Street
Peterborough, NH 03458

> (*The Pueblo Indians, F114, and
> Diné: People of the Navajo
> Nation,* 789; excellent inexpensive
> softcover books with helpful
> teacher's guides)

The Olive Press
5727 Dunmore
W. Bloomfield, MI 48322

> (*Through Indian Eyes: the Native
> American Experience in books for
> children,* 300 pages of thought-evoking
> information and book reviews)

FREE VIDEO AND ACTIVITY GUIDE

Bureau of Land Management
Washington, D.C. 20240

> (*Mystery of the Cliffs,* grades K-4;
> Ninja Turtles teach children the
> idea of stewardship of natural–cultural
> resources; *The Intriguing Past,
> Fundamentals of Archaeology,* grades 4-7:
> includes a teacher's guide and creative
> reproducibles)

FREE WORKSHOP

Project Archaeology
Cindy Ramsay
The Imagination Team/BLM
P.O. Box 758
Dolores, CO 81323

> (This workshop trains teachers of
> grades 4-7 to show children their Nation's
> heritage and cultural history through use
> of public lands. Write for address and date
> of workshop in your state.)

POTTERY BROADSHEETS

The Print Shop
Palace of Governors
Museum of New Mexico
Santa Fe, NM 87501

("Sky Loom" and other Native
American poems, as translated
by Herbert J. Spinden 65 years
ago, on beautiful broadsheets,
four per package)

MAP

National Geographic Society
1145 17th Street, NW
Washington, D.C. 20077-9966

(*"Indians of North America,"*
©1982, #02816; request current
price before ordering)

BIBLIOGRAPHY

PROFESSIONAL BOOKS

Caduto, Michael J. and Bruchac, Joseph. *Keepers of the Earth, Native American Stories and Environmental Activities for Children*. Golden, CO: Fulcrum, Inc., 1988

Doherty, Craig A. and Doherty, Katherine M. *The Apaches and The Navajos*. New York: Franklin Watts, 1992. (Each of these is one of a series and all of these little books are excellent. The series, entitled *Indians of North America*, includes: *The Hopi, The Ute, The Zuni, The Pima-Maricopa, The Yuma*, and *The Pueblo*.)

Fronval, George and Dubois, Daniel. *Indian Symbols and Sign Language*. New York: Bonanza Books, Crown Publishers, 1985.

Iverson, Peter. *The Navajos*. New York: Chelsea House Publishers, 1990

Nabokov, Peter and Easton, Robert. *Native American Architecture*. New York: Oxford University Press, 1989.

Newcomb, Franc Johnson. *Navajo Folktales*. Albuquerque: University of New Mexico Press, 1967.

Ortiz, Alfonso. *The Pueblo*. New York and Philadelphia: Chelsea House Publishers, Mainline Book Co., 1994.

Salinas-Norman, Bobbi. *Indo-Hispanic Folk Art Traditions*. Oakland, CA: Piñata Publications, 1991. (200 Lakeside Drive 94612).

Slapin, Beverly and Seale, Doris. *Through Indian Eyes, The Native Experience in Books for Children*. Philadelphia: New Society Publishers, 1992. (4527 Springfield Avenue, 19143).

Wright, Barton. *Hopi Kachinas, the Complete Guide to Collecting Kachina Dolls*. Flagstaff, AZ: Northland Publishing, 1992. (P.O. Box 1389, 86002).

Yolen, Jane. *Favorite Folktales from Around the World*. New York: Pantheon Books, Random House, 1986.

Young, John V. *Kokopelli, Casanova of the Cliff Dwellers*. Palmer Lake, CO: The Filter Press, 1990.

CHILDREN'S BOOKS

Cohlene, Terri. *Turquoise Boy, A Navajo Legend*. Vero Beach, FL: Watermill Press, The Rourke Corp Inc., 1990.

Copeland, Peter F. *Southwest Indian Coloring Book*. New York: Dover Publications, Inc., 1994.

dePaola, Tomie. *The Legend of the Indian Paintbrush*. New York: Putnam's Sons, 1988.

Hausman, Gerald. *Turtle Dream*. Santa Fe, NM: Mariposa Publishers, 1993. (922 Baca Street, 87501).

Keegan, Marcia. *Pueblo Boy, Growing Up in Two Worlds*. New York: Cobblehill Books, Dutton Publishing Co., 1991.

McDermott, Gerald. *Arrow to the Sun*. New York: Penguin Books, 1974.

Nelson, Mary Carroll. *Michael Naranjo, the Story of an American Indian*. Minneapolis: Dillon Press, 1975. (500 S. Third, 55415).

Powell, Suzanne. *The Pueblos*. New York: Franklin Watts, 1993.

Van Ness, Trysitje. *The Gift of Changing Woman*. New York: Henry Holt & Co., 1993.

Photo 48. Boy fun maker; Hopi, Arizona; circa 1930. *Photo by Witter Bynner. Courtesy Museum of New Mexico (neg. no. 99045).*

Dried Fruit Slices

The Spanish brought fruit trees to the people of the Southwest. They sliced, dried and enjoyed the fruit just as YOU can!

You will need: apples
                 peaches
                 apricots

a serrated knife
a carrot peeler
new (cotton) string
2 tacks or 2 nails and a hammer.

Wash your hands.
Wash the fruit well.
(Peel the peaches if you like.)
Carefully cut each fruit in half. (You may want a grown up to help you with this.) Take out all the seeds. Then carefully cut each fruit half into THIN slices.

Now string the slices on the cotton string. Tack or nail the string up across the room. Make a little space between each slice.

When the fruit is dry take it off the string and ENJOY your Dried Fruit Slices!!

© 1995 Center for Applied Research in Education

NOTES

 NOTES

 NOTES

 NOTES